Making It Work

Career Management
for the
New Workplace

Marilyn Van Norman

BURGHER
BOOKS

Burgher Books
10 Edmund Avenue
Toronto, Ontario
M4V 1H3 Canada

Canadian Cataloguing in Publication Data

Van Norman, Marilyn
    Making it work: career management for the new workplace

Co-published by the Canadian Association of Career Educators and Employers.
Includes bibliographical references and index.
ISBN 1-896176-09-7

1. Career development. 2. Job hunting.
I. Canadian Association of Career Educators and Employers.
II. Title.

HF5381.V35 1995   650.14   C95-932083-0

Distributed by:

Raincoast Books Limited
8680 Camble Street
Vancouver, B.C.
V6P 6M9 Canada
Toll-free order line: 1-800-663-5714

Printed and bound in Canada

95 96 97 98 99 5 4 3 2 1

CONTENTS

Chapter 1: Skills

Chapter 2: Writing A Successful Résumé

Chapter 3: Researching Work Opportunities

Chapter 4: Marketing Yourself

Chapter 5: Managing Your Career

Chapter 1
SKILLS

INTRODUCTION

Change is the operative word when it comes to discussing today's workplace. It is the one constant in the current world of work as we are beginning to know it. Economic realities, technological advances, globalization and demographics are among the forces driving change. It should be noted that the workplace has never been static - it has always been susceptible to change. The difference today is the rate at which change occurs.

In an article in *Engineering Dimensions* called "Jobs With A Future," Nuala Beck and Joseph Connolly talk about the fact that, "The job security of yesteryear has been replaced with the unspoken fear: 'Am I employable in this new economy? Do I have the skills to compete in this high tech world?'"[1] The answer to these questions is a resounding - yes!

In "Jobs With A Future," the authors outlined four common misconceptions about the New Economy. These are:

- *The New Economy is only small business.* In fact, the New Economy comes in all shapes and sizes. Microsoft, Motorola and Spar Aerospace - New Economy players all - are hardly small businesses.

- *The New Economy is a service economy.* Wrong. The New Economy is manufactured goods and services. What are cell phones and computers if not manufactured goods?

1

- *The New Economy is only high-tech.* Although the engines that drive this New Economy are sky-high tech, most of the suppliers to the New Economy aren't.

- *The New Economy is a jobless economy.* Nothing could be further from the truth. Between 1984 and 1993, Canada's New Economy created 816,065 new jobs.

There are countless opportunities available in today's market for college and university graduates who understand their skills, continue to develop them, know how to market them and know what is happening in the new workplace.

"The Fit is Everything" was a recent headline in a research firm's newspaper ad. Understanding the fit between your skills and the work opportunities available is everything! Well, almost everything - understanding the changes that have occurred and continue to occur in the workplace is also key to your success.

THE NEW WORKPLACE

The workplace of the 1990s and beyond will resemble less and less that of previous decades. In the '50s, '60s and '70s, people looking for work assumed they would find what was until recently called a permanent job. Only half the people looking for work in the '90s will find continuing work, much less a permanent job. The other half will be either self-employed or will work in a part-time, temporary, contract or consulting capacity. This percentage will continue to grow as we move into the twenty-first century.

Technological advances are primarily responsible for this dramatic shift. Far from being depressing, this progression offers tremendous opportunities to those who are prepared. The best preparation is education and the ongoing development of skills. It's also important to be able to identify your skills and determine which ones you would like to use in a work setting. The next section will help you do this.

Skills Assessment

In an age of uncertainty, one fact is clear. You, as a college or university graduate, have myriad skills that will be helpful to any number of potential employers. Work opportunities are created daily for highly skilled individuals and 1993 Statscan numbers attest to this fact:

- 308,000 more jobs in Canada for university graduates (up 17% from 1990)
- 170,000 more jobs for college graduates (up 5% from 1990)
- 16,000 fewer jobs for those with a high school diploma
- 651,000 fewer jobs for those who *failed to graduate from high school*

And this was in 1993 - in the middle of a devastating recession. What makes a college or university graduate so marketable? There is really only one answer - skills.

In the first part of this book you will learn how to identify your skills and experiences, then discover which work opportunities they might fit. You'll learn to highlight those skills in a powerful résumé and covering letters, and you'll learn to effectively market them to potential employers.

Types of Skills

Skills may be broken down into three categories: personal; transferable; work/knowledge specific. Personal skills are those that make you who you are. They are the words friends would use to describe you. Transferable skills have been developed through your schooling, paid and volunteer work experience and extracurricular activities and may be used in any setting. Work/knowledge specific skills are normally developed through specific education/training programs and experience.

Skills Identification

Begin to assess your career management plans by identifying your skills. Whether this is the first time you have ever done it, or you have been working for a while and are thinking about changing positions or the type of work you do, skills identification is a must. The following exercise will help you identify your personal and transferable skills.

In each section, circle the skills you think you have. Do not be modest.

Personal skills

humor	sensitivity	self-confidence
warmth	sincerity	reliability
honesty	integrity	positivism
initiative	energy	ethics
drive	determination	loyalty
respect for diversity	accountability	co-operation
risk taking	inner strength	maturity
vitality	enthusiasm	intelligence
responsibility	thoughtfulness	athleticism
assertiveness	vision	global thinking
attention to details	depth	optimism
physical fitness	diversified interests	

This is not an exhaustive list, so add any personal skills you feel you have.

Transferable Skills

thinking critically	researching
analyzing	organization
listening	reading with comprehension
presentation	problem solving
creativity	decision making
mathematical ability	language ability
computer internet	knowledge of e-mail
goal setting	time management
team work	teaching
demonstrating	training
design	leadership
delegating	persuasion
negotiation	debating
influencing	selling
coaching	co-ordinating
motivation	evaluating
testing	setting priorities
information gathering	program development
budgeting	artistic ability
musical ability	acting
writing	assembling
building	operating equipment
management	troubleshooting
interviewing	promoting
observation	scheduling
financial planning	adaptability
positive attitude	communicating effectively

Circle the transferable skills you think you have. Add any others.

Work/Knowledge Specific Skills

List your work/knowledge specific skills. Examples might include:

laboratory	computer programming
languages	systems analysis
LAN management	telemarketing
public relations	benefits/compensation
accounting	psychological testing
interior design	emergency nursing
social research	translation
waste management	strength testing
word processing	travel consulting
policy analysis	drafting
field-testing	psychometric readings
commercial baking	graphic design
newsletter-writing	jewelry-making

Prioritize Your Skills

We all have skills we enjoy using during our personal time but would prefer not to use in a work situation. Look at your list of skills and cross out those that, although you are proud to have, are not ones you would like to use in a work setting.

Summary of Your Skills

List the five skills circled in each of the previous exercises which you would most like to use in a work setting.

Personal Skills

_____

_____

_____

_____

_____

Transferable Skills

_____

_____

_____

_____

_____

Work/Knowledge Specific Skills

_____

_____

_____

_____

_____

SKILL GROUPINGS

The following list represents groupings of skills that have been identified from a number of sources. Examine this list and mark the skills you have identified as having and wanting to use. After completing this exercise, you will be able to tell at a glance which groups of skills best represent your talents and abilities. The groups you identify are the skill sets you will use in writing your résumé. You'll use them as headings in a skills-based résumé format, as foundations for your research into work opportunities, and to market yourself to potential employers.

Analytical

analyze and evaluate	classify
estimate and appraise	examine
research	assess
trouble shoot	investigate

Communications

buy	correspond
distribute	edit
interpret and translate	read and proofread
represent and recruit	promote/sell
write correspondence/materials	listen
public speaking	negotiate
exchange ideas	speak multiple languages

Creative

arrange and display	design
perform	compose
generate new ideas	invent
visualize new concepts	decorate
write poetry, plays, novels	
sketch, paint and photography	

Interactive

coach	direct
tutor	counsel and advise
interview	mediate
public interaction	teach
train	manage
supervise	motivate

Organizational

manage	plan
recordkeeping	co-ordinate
time management	systems development
arrange	delegate
program development	event planning
schedule	administer
decision making	

Physical

athletics	construct
protect	repair
operate	plant
drive	mechanics
restore	

Computational/processing information

quantitative	budget
monitor	balance
estimate	survey
measure	inspect
bookkeep	calculate
data process	

Scientific

laboratory	medical
measure	treat
diagnose	collect
analyze	

Skills Savings Account

All the skills you have identified are now ready to be put in your **skills savings account** to be drawn on whenever appropriate. They are your security, your safety net, results of your wise investments to date. You will want to continue to build on those savings by adding skills to the account on an ongoing basis.

Skills to be Acquired

By doing this exercise, you have probably been able to identify additional skills you would like to develop. Think about which those might be and list them. Beside each skill, indicate how you think it might be acquired. For instance, would you be able to develop a skill through paid work or volunteer experience, through a college or university course or program, through a training program or on your own?

Skills you would like to develop

_____

_____

_____

_____

_____

How you would acquire them

_____

_____

_____

_____

_____

_____

_____

Skills on Employers' Most Wanted List

A recent survey of job listings at the University of Toronto indicated the following skills were required by the majority of employers regardless of the type of work for which an individual was being hired:

- Computer software literacy
- Written and verbal communication
- Interpersonal ability
- Organization
- Analysis and problem solving
- Team work
- Flexibility and Adaptability
- Language
- Juggling multiple tasks and meeting deadlines

Are these skills part of your skills savings account? If not, you might want to consider developing them. An additional skill that should be added to this list is a positive attitude. While many other skills may be learned, attitude is something only you can control. Employers look for people who are enthusiastic and have a positive attitude towards work. We should all do an attitude check from time to time.

Entrepreneurial Skills

Entrepreneurial skills have never been in as much demand in Canada as they are today. Whether you utilize these skills in self-employment, as a contract worker or within an organization, you will profit from them in today's marketplace.

The Bank of Montreal, in co-operation with the Center for Creative Leadership in San Diego, surveyed 264 Canadian entre-

preneurial companies to find out which skills were most important, which were most practised and which skills are statistically
linked to success.[2]

What entrepreneurs say are most important:

> communication
> customer/vendor relations
> listening
> planning
> marketing

What entrepreneurs say they practice most:

> ethics
> self-motivation
> trade and industry knowledge
> customer/vendor relations
> leadership

What skills are statistically linked to success:

> self-motivation/vision
> trade and industry knowledge
> organizing
> marketing
> customer/vendor relations

The article noted that knowing your trade and industry was
critical for startup. Yet once the company took off, self-motivation and organization were key. A smaller U.S. survey showed
that while vision was the most valued skill, financial management was most important for success.

In early 1995, *Ontario Prospects* asked the following question of
potential entrepreneurs: Do you have what it takes to be an
entrepreneur? Give serious thought to your answer. Although
you may decide you wish to gain more experience before strik-
ing out on your own, do not rule out the possibility of someday
being self-employed.

EXPERIENCE ASSESSMENT

Just as it is essential to assess your skills, it is equally important to assess your experiences. In so doing, you will be identifying skills developed through paid work experience, and through volunteer experience, through activities and interests, and through participation in professional associations and the community.

Trish's Story

Trish Billings, who is about to graduate, was asked to outline her experiences to demonstrate the art of experience assessment. To get started, Trish was asked to list all the relevant experiences she could think of in which she had been involved over the past five years. Trish's list looked like this:

- camp counsellor
- salesperson at Sporting Life
- cashier at Sporting Life
- receptionist at Brawley Cathers Ltd.
- market researcher
- skied at Whistler
- traveled around Europe
- did volunteer work at a children's mental health agency
- sold daffodils for the Cancer Society
- took part in Shinerama
- student membership in the Toronto chapter of the Canadian Marketing Association
- attended aerobics classes
- read
- visited art galleries
- did some gourmet cooking

What Skills Were Developed?

Trish consulted her skills savings account to determine what
primary skills had been developed and used in each experience.

Experience	Skills
camp counselor	interpersonal, warmth, humor, time management, organization, respect for diversity, problem solving, teaching, motivating, speaking French, athletic
salesperson	interpersonal, assertive, self- confidence, influencing, communication, listening, persuasion, promoting
cashier	mathematical, decision making, interpersonal, communication, observation, keyboard, humor, patience, time management, balancing
receptionist	interpersonal, communication, juggling multiple tasks, word processing, problem solving, listening, working under pressure, speaking French
market research	analysis, research, data entry, interviewing, listening, communication, critical thinking, organization
skiing	athletic, risk taking, humor, self-confidence, optimism
traveling	communication, languages, problem solving, respect for diversity
volunteer work	interpersonal, teaching, motivating, selling, persuading
interests	athletic, artistic, interpersonal relationships, reading, investments

By completing this exercise, Trish developed a clear idea of her skills and how they were utilized in her various experiences. Her skills and experiences, coupled with her academic background, will form the foundation of her résumé and the content of her covering letters. Now that she has assessed her skills and experiences, Trish is ready to begin to relate what she has to offer to possible work opportunities.

Your Turn - Experience Assessment

With your skills list beside you, complete the following exercises:

List your experiences over the past five years

_____

_____

_____

_____

_____

_____

Which Skills Were Developed?

Experience   Skills

_____   _____

_____   _____

_____   _____

_____   _____

_____   _____

_____   _____

_____   _____

Experience   Skills

_____   _____

_____   _____

_____   _____

_____   _____

_____   _____

_____   _____

_____   _____

You, too, are now ready to write an impressive résumé, and to begin to link your skills and experiences to possible work opportunities. However, before you set out to look for employment, it is extremely important to understand what is happening in the workplace of today. The next section will discuss the rapidly changing world of work and potential growth areas.

AREAS OF GROWTH IN TODAY'S EMPLOYMENT MARKET

The world of work is changing rapidly, and with that change, exciting career opportunities are emerging. Growth areas call for a clear definition of skills and experiences. Assessing your skills and being able to relate them to both past and future experiences gives you a competitive edge when you are seeking employment.

Do not be limited to the applicability of your particular academic background when you consider work. For instance, even though you do not have a technical degree or diploma, your combination of influencing, negotiating, persuasion, language and leadership skills may be exactly what a computer firm is looking for in a salesperson. Read the following description of emerging trends with this in mind.

Technological

In the past 25 years, computer technology has affected almost every occupation to some degree. Today, there is a particular need for individuals with skills to meet the following opportunities:

systems analysts	hardware designers
software developers	researchers
marketing/salespeople	designers
trainers	internet experts
telecommunications	word processing experts
data entry clerks	purchasing agents

database administrators

Local Area Network administrators

interactive learning developers

financial analysts/accountants

Do you have skills and interests that might match these areas? List them.

_____   _____

_____   _____

_____   _____

_____   _____

_____   _____

_____   _____

_____   _____

_____   _____

Global Competition

As a result of the global economy, technological advancements and declines in tariff protection, Canadian organizations are exploring methods to reduce costs, increase productivity and improve quality. There is a demand for employees with relevant skills in the following areas.

telecommunications	marketing and sales
distribution	transportation
international law	international development
internet	quality control
finance	engineering
travel industry	multiple languages
knowledge of different cultures	
international work and life experience	

Do you have skills and interests that might match these areas? List them.

_____	_____
_____	_____
_____	_____
_____	_____
_____	_____
_____	_____
_____	_____

Demographic Changes

Canadians are aging! Between 1991 and 2036, as baby boomers reach retirement, the number of Canadians over the age of 65 will increase from 3.2 million to an astounding 8.6 million. This aging population will require products and services to meet its needs. We tend to think initially of health care products and services, but opportunities are not limited to this area. As the baby boomers age, they will be spending some of the money they have been making over the years, so the demand for cottages, travel, recreational facilities and personal services, just to name a few potential growth areas, will increase. Examples of growth areas include:

health care	health care equipment
home care	nursing homes
seniors' residences	diagnostic techniques
alternative health care	retirement counselling
travel agencies/guides	recreational activities
rural real estate	financial counselling

Do you have skills and interests that might match these areas? List them.

_____   _____
_____   _____
_____   _____
_____   _____
_____   _____
_____   _____

Environmental Issues

As most of us know only too well, our planet is deteriorating at a rapid rate. Toxic waste, acid rain, pollution, the overuse of natural resources and inefficient use of electricity are but a few of the major problems we face. Opportunities are likely to grow for people who can match their skills to these areas:

environmental engineering	environmental law
waste management	water treatment
recycling	reforestation

pollution control	public education/training
Third World development	policy development
wetlands experts	international development
advocates	community development

writing for journals, magazines, newspapers

Do you have skills and interests that might match these areas? List them.

_____	_____
_____	_____
_____	_____
_____	_____
_____	_____
_____	_____

The only limitation to entry into these growing fields is the inability to see where your skills might fit. In addition to skills specific to the area, all industries require: financial, human resources, purchasing, advertising, marketing/sales, writers, trainers, public relations, media relations and lawyers, to name just a few skills sets. Do not limit yourself: your academic background may not be in the health field, but you may find employment opportunities in that area.

PREPARING FOR CHANGE

We have heard many references to changes in the workplace. What are those changes? William Bridges, in his much quoted book, *Job Shift*, talks about today's organization "being transformed from a structure built out of jobs to a field of work needing to be done." As the nature of work changes, jobs, job titles and job descriptions have become outmoded, according to Bridges. They are "rigid solutions to an elastic problem." This is a significant change not only in the way work is structured, but in the way individual workers will see themselves.

Bridges sees three essential characteristics for success in the new workplace:

- employability - attractive to employers e.g. having the abilities and attitudes an employer needs at the moment
- vendor-mindedness - e.g. think like an external vendor who has been hired to accomplish a specific task
- resilience - ability to bend, let go of outdated approaches, learn new approaches

Canadian recruitment practices in the '90s bear out what Bridges is saying. "Just in time hiring" is one of the phrases frequently used by today's employers as they look for the individual who has the abilities and attitudes they need right now. More and more organizations are hiring on a contract or part-time basis. They are hiring people to do a specific task. We know from our research that employers in today's market are looking for individuals who are innovative, flexible and committed to learning - who have the ability to bend, let go of outdated approaches and continue learning.

Employability, Vendor-mindedness and Resilience

The new workplace is one of evolving structure, one in which traditional beliefs in job security, dreams of "climbing the corporate ladder", choosing a career and being in it the rest of your working life, no longer fit; one in which small or medium-sized businesses may attract more applicants than governments or large organizations.

The new workplace is evolving as you read this book. No one is absolutely sure of its direction, but we do know that skills and change are integral components.

Janis Foord Kirk, in the *Toronto Star*'s "Career Monitor," stated,

"It has been said that most of us possess well over 500 skills. Many of them are so much a part of our nature that we are hardly aware of them."[3] This is absolutely true. However, becoming aware of them and beginning to understand how to relate them to potential opportunities is the first step in effective career development.

The most important investment you will ever make is the one you make in yourself. Remember: identify, prioritize and group your skills, and continue to develop new skills based on your assessment of workplace needs. Continue to build your skills saving account.

The next step in the process of finding the type of work you want is to learn to write an effective résumé.

Chapter 2

WRITING A SUCCESSFUL RÉSUMÉ

INTRODUCTION

Attaining the skills of writing effective résumés and covering letters will give you a competitive edge in the marketplace. This chapter will introduce the various components of résumé and covering letter writing, provide tips on the advantages of the different formats available and give a wide range of sample résumés and covering letters.

A RÉSUMÉ

- provides the first impression a potential employer has of you
- outlines your skills, education, experience and interests
- profiles your ability to do the work for which an employer is hiring
- highlights your achievements and accomplishments
- gives the employer a sense of who you are
- is used in an interview to clarify skills and experience

What Makes a Résumé Effective?

- skills, education, experiences and achievements are clearly evident

- choice of résumé format works to your advantage
- material used is concise and to the point
- action words are used to describe previous work experience
- presentation is professional, free of spelling and grammatical errors
- layout and appearance are appealing
- clearly and powerfully presents who you are and what you can do
- is relevant to the positions to which you are applying

In an article in the *Globe and Mail*, entitled "Pack Your Resume with Punch," writer Gordon Powers quoted Kathryn Bolt of Robert Half International as saying "A successful resume these days doesn't sell degrees or responsibilities; it talks intimately about accomplishments and matches specific requirements with abilities."[4]   That means you should concentrate on your most significant achievements in past positions.

The Employability Skills Profile: What Are Employers Looking For?

The first step in writing a résumé, whether it is your first or twenty-first, is to assess your skills and determine which ones you would like to highlight.

The Employability Skills Profile: What Are Employers Looking For? is one of the most referred-to career-related documents produced in recent years. It was developed in 1992 by the Conference Board of Canada after interviewing employers across Canada and asking them what skills, attitudes and behaviors they most value in an employee.

Academic Skills

- understand and speak languages in which business is conducted
- listen to, understand and learn
- read, comprehend and use written materials, including graph charts and displays

- write effectively in the languages in which business is conducted
- think critically and act logically to evaluate situations, solve problems and make decisions
- understand and solve problems involving mathematics and use the results
- use technology, instruments, tools and information systems effectively
- access and apply specialized knowledge from various fields (e.g. skilled trades, technology, physical sciences, arts and social sciences)
- continue to learn for life

Personal Management Skills

- self-esteem and confidence
- honesty, integrity and personal ethics
- a positive attitude toward learning, growth and personal health
- initiative, energy and persistence to get the job done
- the ability to set goals and priorities in work and personal life
- the ability to plan and manage time, money and other resources to achieve goals
- accountability for actions taken
- a positive attitude toward change
- recognition of and respect for people's diversity and individual differences
- the ability to identify and suggest new ideas to get the job done - creativity

Teamwork Skills

- understand and contribute to an organization's goals
- understand and work within culture of the group
- plan and make decisions with others and support the outcomes
- respect the thoughts and opinions of others in the group
- exercise give and take to achieve group results
- seek a team approach as appropriate
- lead when appropriate, mobilizing the group for high performance

BASIC RÉSUMÉ COMPONENTS

Résumés normally are comprised of the following sections:

Personal Information

This section typically appears at the top of the resume and includes the following:

- Name
- Address - be sure to use the address from which you will be looking for work
- Telephone number - give the number where you may be reached or where a message may be left
- E-mail address or fax number, if applicable

In Canada, it is against the law for an employer to ask for information such as sex, age, marital status, height, weight, race, religion or political belief. It is advisable not to include this information in your résumé.

Career Objective

Many employers prefer to see a clearly stated career objective at the beginning of a résumé. An example of a specific objective might be: "A fashion design position specializing in children's clothes," or "To work on an electrical engineering project in a developing country." It is not advisable to include a career objective if by doing so you feel you would limit response to your résumé. You might choose instead to include your career objectives in your covering letters.

Education

- Begin with most recent education

- Employers prefer to see dates on the left hand side
- State degree/diploma, area of study, educational institution, year
- Mention GPA, if outstanding
- Give thesis title and/or topic, if pertinent
- Relevant Courses - list key courses if pertinent
- Awards - include scholarships, bursaries and recognized accomplishments
- Computer Skills - list software and programming languages with which you are familiar
- Language Skills - list languages and proficiency in oral and written form

Work Experience - Used in a Chronological Résumé Format

The following information is usually presented in this section:

- Dates of employment - employers prefer to have these listed on the left-hand side and in reverse chronological order.
- Position title in **bold**
- Name and location of the employer
- List of skills, responsibilities and accomplishments
- List of significant contributions

Skills and Accomplishments - Used in a Skills-Based Résumé Format

- Skills sets - group the skills in headings you know are most relevant to the position to which you are applying (e.g. communication, public relations, fund-raising, marketing)
- Describe the responsibilities and accomplishments, with reference to where the skills were used
- Include a brief work history following the skill set headings - date, position title, organization, location
- Include volunteer experience

- State accomplishments, e.g. Placed first in Vancouver High School Science Contest; Named Employee of the Month at NDB Industries; Increased sales at Sporting World by 15%

Guidelines for Work Experience and Skills and Accomplishments Sections

- Use action words to describe the work you did - analyzed, directed, implemented, increased, designed, initiated, tested, verified, wrote
- Use active rather than passive voice to describe experience
- Do not use personal pronouns
- Be direct, positive and honest
- Be straightforward and simple
- Include relevant volunteer work
- Use the appropriate tense to describe the experience

Activities and Interests

- Skills such as leadership, organization and interpersonal are often demonstrated in this section
- Include club and professional association membership, campus activities, hobbies and sports
- List volunteer experiences if you have not included these under the Work Experience section
- Indicate whether positions were elected or appointed
- Articulate level of responsibility, skills used and accomplishments

References

Include this sentence in your résumé:

- *References will be supplied upon request.*

Always be sure to ask permission to use the names of your references beforehand, and give them a copy of your résumé. You obviously want to be relatively sure what your references might say about you before you give their names to a prospective employer.

Additional Headings

- Summary of Qualifications
- Additional Skills
- Special Skills
- Related Experience
- Presentations
- Publications
- Advanced Training
- Volunteer Experience
- Demonstrated Skills/Abilities
- Memberships/Professional Affiliations

List of action words to describe responsibilities and previous experience in your résumé:

achieved	categorized	created
administered	classified	dealt with
advised	coached	decided
analyzed	coded	defined
answered	collected	delegated
applied	communicated	demonstrated
arranged	completed	designed
assembled	composed	developed
assessed	computed	devised
assigned	conducted	edited
began	constructed	encouraged
bought	contacted	established
built	contributed	estimated
calculated	coordinated	evaluated
cared for	counselled	explained

gathered	memorized	responded
generated	modified	retrieved
guided	motivated	reviewed
handled	negotiated	revised
helped	operated	searched
identified	ordered	selected
illustrated	organized	simplified
implemented	outlined	sold
improved	perceived	spoke
increased	performed	succeeded
initiated	persuaded	summarized
instructed	planned	supported
interacted	prepared	synthesized
interpreted	printed	taught
invented	produced	tested
led	promoted	trained
listened	recorded	tutored
located	regulated	used
managed	repaired	united
manipulated	represented	verified
measured	reorganized	volunteered
mediated	researched	wrote

RÉSUMÉ FORMATS

Chronological Format

This is the format preferred by most employers, as they are able to see at a glance your education and experience and when they were attained. Education and work history are listed in reverse chronological order, starting with the most recent. This format appeals to résumé-writers with a consistent work history in positions with progressive responsibilities.

Advantages

- the preferred format of most employers
- allows a quick summary of education and experience

- shows at a glance progressive responsibilities and skill development

Modified Chronological Format

This format allows you to group or highlight work experiences while maintaining reverse chronological order. Relevant experiences or categories of experience may be emphasized by listing them first.

Advantages

- helpful when applying to employers in the same field where experience has been attained
- allows the employers' attention to be focused on key work experience

Skills-Based (Modified Functional) Format

The skills-based format lets you highlight groups of skills and provides the employer with a listing in reverse chronological order of work experience. The skills listed support your career or work objective. When listing a skill or accomplishment, refer to the respective position title and organization.

Advantages

- lets you highlight the skills most relevant to the position being sought
- lets you include skills developed through extracurricular and volunteer work, and other interests
- lets you present skills developed and used in work experiences not directly related to current employment goals
- effective if there are gaps in employment history or if you have limited work experience

Creative Format

The creative format may be appropriate when you apply for positions that call for individuality and creativity. In this format, there is no standard approach. A word of caution - before you choose to use a creative format for your résumé be sure to research its appropriateness.

Advantages

- allows artistic, literary and creative skills to be illustrated
- may be an appropriate format for employers seeking proof of visual or written creativity
- allows for individuality in presentation and style

The Multimedia Resume

An article in the *Globe and Mail* entitled, "CV That Sings," stated, "Today, computer graphic and multimedia artists are skipping paper resumes and portfolios and doing what they do best: putting pictures and information on disk with themselves as the main subject."

Multimedia résumés often follow the same guidelines in terms of headings, description of skills and experience as a more traditional résumé, but come alive via pictures, graphics and music. Architects, advertising people and photographers are beginning to see a new method of presentation for their résumés. By developing an innovative and well-presented résumé on disk, you demonstrate your creativity and your computer ability. In the field of multimedia, it is most often the multimedia résumé that gets seen.

The Electronic Résumé

Some large organizations are using electronic résumé software to scan and search résumés in specialized databases. To be prepared to respond to an employer who requires résumés that may be scanned, you will have to take into consideration the following points:

- use white or off-white paper only
- do not fold or staple your résumé
- do not fax your résumé
- do not use italics, underline, shading or special characters
- may use bold
- use a laser printer
- do not use script or graphics
- may use solid bullets or asterisks
- use a minimum of 10 point type size (12 point is preferable)
- avoid double columns
- send originals only
- use traditional résumé structure
- ensure that your name is the first text on the résumé
- use nouns instead of verbs to indicate job titles and skills

SAMPLE RÉSUMÉS

Chronological Format

As both Christopher Wong's and Jodie Winfrey's experiences have been sequential and have show increasing responsibility and complexity, they chose to use the chronological format. Their résumés appear on the following pages.

Christopher Wong
1842 Pine Avenue
Vancouver, British Columbia
V6J 3C9
604-555-8729

Career Objective   To secure a position in a comprehensive Management Training Program within the financial community

Education

June 1995   **University of British Columbia**
                 B.A.: Economics/Finance

Skills   Speak Mandarin, Cantonese
                 Proficient in Word, Excel, DBXL Plus
                 90% on VSE Securities Course

Work Experience

Summer 1994   **Research Assistant**
                 Bank of Montreal
                 Vancouver, B.C.

- Conducted research on legal information related to funding accounting, transfer agency and foreign subcustodian agreements
- Created an on-line filing system of all pertinent mutual funds data for general reference
- Developed an index of investor charges through investigation and research of fee schedules
- Systematized and formatted all dates of legal compliance agreements
- Worked independently on a project to originate procedures for more efficient operation of the department

Summer 1993   **Brokers Assistant**
Scotia McLeod
Toronto, ON

- Monitored back office clearance of stock transfers
- Conducted research of TSE companies for profitability determination
- Maintained customer accounts for brokers
- Increased clientele by 10% through cold calls

Summer 1992   **Placement Assistant**
W.B. Walker & Associates
Vancouver, B.C.

- Conducted background investigations of applicants for potential employment by various companies
- Prepared performance evaluations and summarized qualifications of each applicant
- Performed general office functions for the entire office

Activities and Interests

President of the UBC Finance Club
Membership Co-ordinator for Chinese
Students' Association
Volunteer worker for Red Cross
Pitcher for Intramural Baseball Team

Enjoy art, stock market, skiing, tennis

References: **Available upon request**

Jodie Winfrey
4632 Oxford Street
Montréal, Québec
H4A 2Y8
514-555-8016

Career Objective: To work in a responsible and progressively challenging marketing position in an international organization.

Education:

1995	Business Administration Diploma, Marketing Specialty, CEGEP Vanier, Montréal

Skills: Languages: Fluent in French, speak some Italian
            Computer: Word, WordPerfect 6.0, Excel

Employment Experience:

1992 - Present   **Supervisor**
            St. Denis Café, Montréal

> Supervise three employees on the evening shift
>
> Book and confirm reservations
>
> Attend to customer complaints
>
> Perform night cash outs and complete wage cost sheets
>
> Greet customers at the door and seat them
>
> Named Employee of the Month three times in 1994

1990 - 1992   **Assistant Manager**
            Michel's Catering

> Hired and trained servers
>
> Acted as hostess, server and bartender at events
>
> Supervised staff
>
> Brought in $20,000 of business per year

1989 - 1992   **Designer and Owner**
            Jodie's Jewelry

Designed and made unique earrings

Developed business plan

Marketed and sold jewelry at college and craft shows

Netted $2,000 per year

1988 - 1989   **Usher**
Expos Baseball Club

Greeted fans and showed them to their seats

Dealt with disturbances

1987 - 1988   **Server**
Dairy Queen

Dealt with the public in an efficient and courteous manner

Weekend supervisor of 3 - 4 staff

Volunteer Work

1993   Co-ordinator
Vanier College Blood Drive

1989   Volunteer reader
Massey Nursing Home

Achievements

Business Administration Honour role

Vice-President, Marketing Club

President of High School Junior Achievement

Nominated for Terry Fox Award

Captain of Vanier Field Hockey Team

Provincial Badminton Champion

Won both high school and college Athletic Letters

Interests: Ringette, badminton, field hockey, reading, art

References: Available upon request

Modified Chronological Format

Catherine Modali is looking for work in the area of environmental science and therefore has chosen to use a modified chronological resume format in order to group her scientific work experience and present it separately from her other experiences.

Catherine Teresa Modali
990 Winwick Road
Halifax, Nova Scotia
B3H 4L5
902-555-6782

Education

1991 - 1995	**B.Sc., Honours Environmental Science** Dalhousie University Main focus: Aquatic Ecology and Fish Biology
Computer Skills	Excel, Word, Windows, SAS
Field Experience	Terrestrial and Freshwater Biology - Algonquin Park Tropical Ecosystems - Costa Rica Marine Biology - Newfoundland Tropical Marine Biology - Bahamas

Relevant Experience

Summer 1994	**Laboratory Technician** Dalhousie University

- Transferred, set up and maintained a microsatellite DNA fingerprinting laboratory at the Halifax Museum
- Gained both administrative and organizational skills
- Honed accuracy skills and developed ability to work independently

1993 - present	**Field and Laboratory Research Assistant** Memorial University

---

- Snorkelled and SCUBA dove as part of extensive field-work project on fish reproductive behaviour
- Collected behavioural data, samples of fish and tagged fish
- Used qualitative and quantitative methods to analyze parasites
- Interacted with academic professionals in the biological field
- Worked as part of an academic team

September 1992 -   **Invigilator**
May 1994   Dalhousie University, Zoology Examinations

- Distributed and supervised first year exams

Other Work Experience

May 1988 -   **Lifeguard and Swimming Instructor**
present   Glenview Swim Club, Toronto

- Organized creative and safe learning environments for swimming lessons
- Developed excellent public relations skills dealing with parents
- Functioned as part of a team in emergency situations

January -   **Fitness Evaluator**
June 1991   St. Clair Fitness Club, Halifax

- Provided exercise and health expertise to new members
- Designed personalized exercise programs

Activities and Interests

- SCUBA License
- Swim team - Gold Medal 1991
- Dalhousie University Campus Beverage Server
- Rock Climbing Club
- Travel, cooking, skiing

References: Available upon request

Skills-Based (Modified Functional) Format

Skills-Based (Modified Functional) Format is Samual's choice, as he would like to emphasize the technical skills he has developed through both his academic and work experiences.

Samual S. Britton
23 Park Road
Calgary, Alberta
T2G 3Y6
403-555-4956

Education

June 1995	**Mechanical Engineering Diploma** Southern Alberta Institute of Technology **GPA 3.89**

Computer Skills   Fortran, Basic, CAD/CAM, APT, Advanced Manufacturing Word, WP 6.0, Excel

Qualifications

- Strong organizational and analytical skills
- Flexible and adapt easily to new situations
- Enjoy learning and committed to ongoing skill development
- Excellent comunications and interpersonal skills
- Fluent in Spanish

Demonstrated Skills

Technical
- Production of detail drawings of mechanical equipment for course project
- Assisted with the design of mechanical components and specified materials to meet static/dynamic load and stress for Ibiscus Steel Ltd.

- Team leader on project to specify machining operations, production methods and tooling for the manufacture of innovative car wash equipment
- Prepared a quality assurance plan and selected inspection methods and implementation procedures for Ibiscus project
- Applied time and method study techniques to production of centrifugal pump for final year project

Sales
- Researched product availability for clients at the parts department, Canadian Tire
- Increased sales by 20% at Canoe Express
- Named Employee of the month at Canadian Tire
- Responded effectively to client inquiries at Welch's Hardware

Leadership
- Elected President of the Mechanical Engineering Club
- Captain of high school hockey team
- Led a group of Boyscouts on a wilderness weekend

Time Management
- Effectively managed a part-time job, full-time studies, volunteer work and maintained a GPA of 3.89
- Handed in all assignments on time
- Increased sales while training new staff at Canoe Express

Interpersonal
- Displayed tact and diplomacy dealing with Canadian Tire clients
- Commended for professionalism, sensitivity and poise in dealing with a very difficult parts department supplier

- Voted most popular student in high school graduating class

Work Experience

Summer 1994   **Assistant to Project Manager**
Ibiscus Steel Ltd., Calgary, Alberta

1992 - Present   **Parts Department Salesperson**
Part-time   Canadian Tire, Calgary, Alberta

Summer 1991   **Salesperson**
Canoe Express, Calgary, Alberta

Summer 1990   **Salesperson**
Welch's Hardware, Calgary, Alberta

Interests and Activities

- President, Mechanical Engineering Club
- Assistant BoyScout Leader
- Intramural Hockey
- Student member of Mechanical Engineering Association

- Enjoy tennis, squash, hiking, painting and auto repair

References   Available upon request

The Skills-Based (Modified Functional) résumé is Sasha Usher's choice in terms of format, as she would like to highlight her acting, stage management and technical experiences.

Sasha Usher
20 Glen Elm Avenue
Toronto, Ontario
M4T 1T7
416-555-4000
FAX 555-3002

Career Objective: To attain a position in a community theatre where it is possible to utilize and further develop acting, directing and stage management skills

Special Skills

> Dialects: Cockney, Irish, French, German, British, American
> Voice and Repertory - 3 years
> Dance: Ballet, Jazz, Modern - 10 years of lessons
> Singing lessons 6 years, alto
> Competetive swimmer
> Cyclist
> Provincially ranked squash player

Accomplishments

> Voted Actress of the Year, York University, 1993
> Chosen to sing in the Canadian choir entry in the 1992 International Choir Festival
> Honour Role in the Drama Department 1992 - 1995
> Kinsman Scholarship 1991
> Nominated for the Terry Fox Award 1990

Acting   **Selected roles at York University**
> Maggie, *Cat on a Hot Tin Roof*
> Ladie Wishfort, *The Way of the World*
> Queen Agravin, *Once Upon a Mattress*
> Glenna, *Edmond*
> Nikki, *Runaways*
> Gertrude Stein, *Chamber Music*

Directing	**York University**
	Director, *Stand By Me*
	Director, *Ikke Ikke Nye Nye Nye*
	Director, *As You Like It*

Stage Management

Summer Stock, Red Barn Theatre
Jackson's Point, Ontario
Assistant Stage Manager, *South Pacific*
Stage Manager, *What the Hell*
Stage Manager, *Godspell*
Stage Manager, *Spring Thaw*

Technical	**Dalhousie University**
	Design/Construction, *Street Scene*
	Design/Lights, *Dance Theatre*
	Makeup, *The Gondoliers*
	Technician, *Runaways*
	Technician, *Edmund*

Administrative

Box Office Manager, National Shakespeare
Festival
Co-ordinator, Toronto Island Summer Theatre
Publicity Assistant, Chester Summer Theatre
Administrative Assistant, Registrar's Office,
Dalhousie University

Education

1992 - 1995	**Honours B.A., Drama, English**
	York University
	Magna Cum Laude

Interests	Squash, Tennis, Sailing, Antiques, Art
References	Available upon request

Richard Rumeo also chose to use a Skills-Based (Modified Functional) résumé format, as he wished to make a career change and wanted to focus on more recently attained skills and education.

Richard Rumeo
111 Bristol Road
Mississauga, Ontario
L4Z 3P6
905-555-5643
FAX 905-555-8972
E-Mail 73560@Compuserve.com

Career Objective: To work as a senior trainer specializing in technology for small businesses in a cutting-edge international training organization.

Qualifications

- Proven training and motivational ability
- Strong interpersonal, organizational and leadership skills
- Proven ability to motivate and coach others
- Creative thinker and problem solver
- Excellent presentation skills
- Well organized, resourceful and flexible
- Fluent in English, French and Spanish
- Excellent knowledge of Word, Excel, WP 6.0, E-Mail, Internet

DEMONSTRATED SKILLS

Technological Training/Presentations

- Designed and taught *Introduction to Computers* courses to ABC Inc. executives
- Designed and taught *Introduction to Microsoft Office* courses to entry level senior managers

---

- Designed and taught *Advanced Word* courses for the University of Toronto Continuing Studies Department 1993 - present
- Presented at the NYU 1995 Conference on *Get Ready - Technology Is Here To Stay*
- Presented at the Canadian Import/Export Conference on *Getting the Most from Technology*
- Presented at the Canadian Bankers Association Conference on *We Have Only Just Begun: A Look at the Technology of the Future*

Additional Teaching Skills

- Taught Grades 10 and 11 math for four years at Toronto Northern High School
- Voted Teacher of the Year each year
- Coach a contending midget All Star Baseball team

Motivational Training/Presentations

- Delivered *Small Business: Big Dreams* presentation to the Ontario Association of Small Businesses
- Designed and taught courses on *Staying Motivated Even When Profits Are Down for the Peel Business Association*

Marketing Skills

- Successfully marketed self-designed courses and presentations in order to pay way through graduate school
- Built a small business from $280,000 in sales to $600,000 in three years

EMPLOYMENT PROFILE

1992 - 1995	Founder and President
	Rumeo & Associates Training Inc.
1988 - 1992	Owner and President
	Safety Supplies Inc.

| 1984 - 1988 | Teacher, Grades 10 and 11 |
| | Toronto Northern High School |

EDUCATION

1995	M.Ed., Adult Education
	Ontario Institute for Educational Studies
1983 - 1984	B.Ed, Secondary
	Queen's University
1979 - 1983	B.A., Commerce
	University of Toronto

INTERESTS Skiing, painting, tennis, camping, trekking

REFERENCES Available upon request

Final Notes on Résumé Writing

- Spend time identifying and grouping your skills
- Choose the format that best fits your needs and that shows your skills most effectively
- Make a list of your skills, experiences and accomplishments
- Consider each position you have held and analyze the contribution you made
- Include volunteer work, elected offices, athletics, community service, awards and scholarships
- Be concise and to the point in your résumé - cut out unnecessary information
- Tell employers who you are and what you will do for them
- Make sure your résumé is visually appealing and free of spelling mistakes and grammatical errors
- Use only one font, and choose one that is easy to read and looks professional

You have the information you need to write an effective résumé. Pour yourself a cup of coffee or tea and turn on the computer - you are on your way to creating a door-opening résumé. Once your résumé is on paper, the next step is the writing of covering letters.

COVERING LETTER - WHAT IS IT?

A covering letter is a letter written to a potential employer, which accompanies your résumé in response to an advertised position or in speculation of a possible opening. It introduces both you and your résumé, while making the link for the employer between your skills and experiences and the work the employer would like done. It is the first impression an employer has of you.

What the experts say about covering letters

A survey of recruiters published in *Recruitment Today* magazine found that the content and appearance of covering letters are essential components in the hiring process.

The survey revealed:

- 95% of employers consider covering letters important
- 96% were able to tell the difference between a form letter and an original
- 85% were offended when their name was misspelled
- 70% read covering letters thoroughly

COMPONENTS OF A COVERING LETTER

Response to an Advertised Position

Analyze the advertisement

Take note of the description of the work, not simply the job title. Assume that the duties outlined are the ones the employer considers most important, and link your skills and experience directly to them.

Note the qualifications listed

Demonstrate how yours match. If they do not exactly fit, explain why you feel your qualifications are relevant.

Research the organization

Conduct thorough research on the organization so that in your letter you are able to show the employer that you have done your homework.

Address the Letter

The letter should be addressed to the individual who will be doing the interviewing. If no name is given in the advertisement, call the organization and find out to whom the letter should be addressed. Your name and address should appear at the top of the letter.

Introductory paragraph

The introductory paragraph addresses the position to which you are applying, where you heard of the opening and why you are interested in applying.

Middle paragraphs

The middle paragraphs describe your understanding of the position and the organization, while stating how your skills and experience directly relate to them. This is the place in the letter where you might want to highlight the personal and transferable skills you have that you believe the employer may be seeking. You will want to mention extracurricular and volunteer work that have provided skills development, as well as any other training you have had that relates to the requirements of the position.

Explain why you are interested in the position and in the organization.

Final paragraph

The last paragraph indicates your interest in an interview, where you may be contacted and when you plan to follow up.

Signature

Always remember to sign your letter and type your name under your signature.

Speculative Covering Letters

- In the first paragraph, introduce yourself and state the type of position(s) in which you have an interest and why. If you received a lead from someone about a possible opening, refer to the source of the information if you think it would be helpful.

- In the second paragraph, describe your knowledge of the organization and the particular area in which you have an interest. State why you feel your skills and experience would fit the requirements of a potential opening.

- In the third paragraph, make the specific link between your educational background, skills and experience and the position(s) in which you have an interest. Highlight your personal and transferable skills, and state how they will let you contribute to the work the organization does.

- In the final paragraph, express your appreciation to the reader for consideration of your request to meet to discuss the possibility of employment. You might conclude with a sentence in which you list a telephone number where you may be reached and a statement that if you do not hear anything from them by a certain date (usually two weeks), you will follow up with a phone call.

Questions to ask yourself before writing a covering letter

- To whom am I writing this letter?
- Do I have a clear idea of the skills I want to market and the experiences I want to highlight?
- What accomplishments do I want to mention?
- Have I adequately researched the organization and the position? Am I able to make the link with my education, skills and experiences?
- Do I clearly understand the fit between my personal and transferable skills and what I know about the organization and the position?

Sample covering letters

Response to an Advertised position:

Management Trainee

The successful candidate will be given training in all aspects of the business including sales, marketing, finance, trading and investment counselling. The position requires a self-starter, who possesses a strong desire to learn, enthusiasm and energy. Placement upon completion of the training program will be in our Hong Kong office.

Individuals with a commerce or finance degree, experience in the investment or finance industry and proficiency in Cantonese or Mandarin are preferred.

Hands-on PC experience, familiarity with computerized systems and the ability to work in a dynamic, fast-paced, team-oriented environment are mandatory.

Qualified candidates wishing to join a dynamic, aggressive and successful organization are invited to mail or fax résumés to: Rider, Sims & Hardy Inc., at the address or numbers below.

Christopher Wong, whose résumé was seen earlier, was extremely interested in this advertisement. He set out to write a covering letter that would convince Rider, Sims & Hardy he was the candidate they sought. Before writing the letter, he reviewed the ad and related his skills and experience to the following key points:

- self-starter - strong desire to learn - enthusiasm - energy - refer to securities course, research work, increased clientele at Scotia McLeod, UBC Finance Club
- Hong Kong Office - has visited Hong Kong several times - impressed with vitality
- Commerce or Finance Degree - B.A., Economics/Finance
- experience in investment or finance - worked at Bank of Montreal, Scotia McLeod
- proficiency in Cantonese & Mandarin - reference to oral and written
- hands on PC experience - Word, Excel, DBXL Plus
- familiarity with computer systems - on-line filing system (B of M), TSE system
- ability to work in a dynamic, fast-paced team-oriented environment - refer to all work experience re: fast-paced and baseball, plus club re: team
- dynamic, aggressive, successful organization - talk about respect for their reputation and market share

The next step was to call and find out to whom to address the letter. Then Christopher was ready to write his covering letter.

March 2, 1995

Ms Sandra Sims
Managing Partner
Rider, Sims & Hardy Inc.
Canada Place Way
Vancouver, B.C.
V6C 3L5

Dear Ms Sims:

Please accept this letter and attached résumé as my application for the management trainee position recently advertised at the University of British Columbia. I believe that I have the skills, academic background and work experience you are looking for.

I am a self-starter with limitless enthusiasm and energy, as witnessed by my initiative in increasing clientele at Scotia McLeod by 10% through cold calls while successfully doing the summer job I was hired to do. My desire to learn is evident in my university and VSE Securities Course marks, as well as the type of summer positions I have attained. The fact that the training for this position leads to placement in the Hong Kong office is exciting to me. I have visited Hong Kong a number of times and have been most impressed by its vitality. I understand that Rider, Sims & Hardy Inc. is just in the process of establishing its office in Hong Kong, which would allow the successful candidate to be part of the building process.

My B.A. in Economics/Finance, along with my experience as research assistant for the Bank of Montreal and as a brokers assistant at Scotia McLeod, has prepared me for the challenges an investment house has to offer. I have both the ability and the desire to work in a dynamic, fast-paced environment.

I have excellent interpersonal skills, sound organizational and analytical ability, and believe that I have had the opportunity to demonstrate both leadership and team membership skills through my roles as President of the UBC Finance Club, Membership Co-ordinator for the Chinese Students' Association and as a member of my baseball team.

I am extremely interested in the Management Trainee position with your firm and very much look forward to the opportunity of being invited for an interview. I may be reached at 604-555-8729.

Sincerely,

Christopher Wong

Sample Speculative Letter

Catherine Modali, whose résumé was seen earlier, is about to launch a letter-writing campaign to environmental consulting firms whose names she has taken from a recently released directory, as well as to contacts she has made during her research. Her letter follows.

May 15, 1995

Dr. Ronald West
Research Director
Canadian Environmental Consultants
375 University Avenue
Toronto, Ontario,
M5G 2J5

Dear Dr. West:

Dr. Wendy Sprout of Fisheries Canada suggested I contact you to inquire about possible openings in your firm for a recent Honours Environmental Science graduate from Dalhousie University. I understand that the focus of one of your firm's research is Fish Conservation and that you have recently received a federal government grant. The focus of my degree has been Aquatic Ecology and Fish Biology and I have had extensive international field work experience

My research indicates that Canadian Environmental Consultants reputation is world-renowned in the area of fish conservation. The most recent turbot crisis reaffirms the importance of your work, and I feel that I have a contribution to make to it.

My field experience in Algonquin Park, Costa Rica, Newfoundland and the Bahamas coupled with my position as field and laboratory research assistant at Memorial University have given a depth of understanding and skill level I think you might find interesting.

I have excellent research, analytical and interpersonal skills. I have worked as part of an academic team and also have proven my ability to work independently. I have a thirst for knowledge and a sound understanding of the importance of continually upgrading my skills.

I would very much appreciate the opportunity of meeting with you to discuss my potential contribution to Canadian Environmental Consultants. I will call during the week of May 30, 1995, to follow-up this letter.

Sincerely,

Catherine Modali

Review

You are now ready to write or rewrite your résumé and begin to produce powerful covering letters. Remember that your résumé and covering letter are often the first impression a potential employer has of you, so make them count. Allocate an adequate amount of time for writing them, and have them critiqued by someone who has had considerable experience hiring.

Make your résumé and covering letters come alive! The reader should, after reading them, have an excellent sense of who you are and what you have to offer. The reader should be able to quickly see how well you would fit into the organization and the possible contributions you would make.

Powerful résumés and covering letters open employment doors. You have the skills employers want. It is up to you to present them in their most favourable light.

A final tip on preparing a powerful résumé and covering letters - no matter how impressive the content of your résumé and covering letter may be, if there are spelling or grammatical errors, if the layout is poor or if the letter is addressed to To Whom It May Concern rather than to the appropriate person, you are unlikely to be asked for the interview. So pay attention to these details and produce the most professional documents you know how. They are, after all, an important investment in your future.

The ultimate goal of writing a strong résumé and covering letter is to be invited for an interview and be offered a position.

In the next chapter - doing your research.

Chapter 3

RESEARCHING WORK OPPORTUNITIES

THE NEW WORKPLACE

The new workplace bares little resemblance to the one your parents and grandparents knew. Not only are the days of working for one organization for 40 years long gone, many of those organizations are gone, as well. For many people, job and retirement security may not be a part of their experience. In fact, the very word "job" is in many experts' opinions on its way out, as well, to be replaced by the concept of piece-work for a specific project.

What does this mean for people at the start of their careers? What does it mean for those who may have enjoyed job security in the past, but who may now be experiencing the frightening prospect of a new world of work?

It means the chance to introduce significantly more flexibility, diversity, entrepreneurialism, independence and self-reliance into you career and life. No, there will not be the same type of security or reliance on an organization previous generations knew, but there will be a greater focus on self-managed careers, quality of life issues and change - frequent change. It also means understanding what the changes are and what their effect on you might be.

An examination of workplace changes indicates that:

- Skills sets are rapidly changing
- Skills development -- including personal, work content and transferability -- is key to success in the new workplace
- There is a clear move to a service-based economy
- Work will be increasingly self-created and will replace the traditional job
- There is a need for new definitions of success
- Contract work and part-time or temporary work are replacing permanent employment
- People will have multiple careers and think of themselves as independent workers
- Work will go to those who are best qualified and can best market themselves
- Flex-time, working from home, invisible offices and job sharing are increasing
- The generalist, particularly one with multiple languages and familiarity with computers, has a new place in the market
- The Information Highway will revolutionize how work is done
- Borders are continuing to shrink, resulting in increased international opportunities
- Entrepreneurialism is coming into its own in Canada
- Ongoing training and education are essential to survival in the new workplace.
- Diversity is challenging the status quo

How Will You Prepare for the New Workplace?

The new workplace is characterized by one constant - change! As William Bridges, in his book *Managing Transitions: Making the Most of Change*, stated, "Change is not the same as transition. Change is situational: the new site, the new boss, the new team, the new policy. Transition is the psychological process people go through to come to terms with the new situation. Change is external, transition is internal." He went on to say that unless transition occurs, change will not happen. Learning to adapt to new situations is essential to thriving in the new workplace.

Preparing for entry to or survival in the new workplace will involve a number of strategies. Among them:

- A commitment to the continued upgrading of skills
- Ongoing analysis of skills and how they match what is required
- Accepting the fact that change is inevitable and learning to adapt quickly
- Being flexible, taking risks
- Developing and being able to effectively market a strong set of skills
- Continually upgrading computer skills
- Learning additional languages
- Exploring opportunities with small and medium-sized organizations
- Developing entrepreneurial skills
- Fine tuning skills employers might want to rent
- Research, research, research, research, research!

RESEARCHING WORK OPPORTUNITIES

"The old adage that knowledge is power is especially true when conducting a job search."

> Dr. Ronald Krannich, *Careering and Re-Careering for the '90s*

Learning how to effectively research work opportunities is a skill that will serve you throughout your working life. Too many new graduates think that looking for work simply involves registering with their college or university career centre and looking at the employment listings. Although certainly an important piece of the process, monitoring the career centre is only a small part. Effective research of work opportunities involves gathering, analyzing and effectively using information. Knowledge is power!

Researching work opportunities involves learning a new set of skills. You will be conducting library research as well as developing interview, electronic and observation skills.

ASSESSING SKILLS, INTERESTS, VALUES, EXPERIENCE AND PREFERRED WORK ENVIRONMENT

At this stage of your career development you might want to think about what is important to you, what you enjoy and, equally important, what you do not like. You might want to begin by asking yourself some questions.

Skills

From the list of skills you identified in chapter 1, which five skills would you like to be able to use in your next work setting? List them. Remember to include skills from all three categories - personal, transferable and work/knowledge specific.

Personal   Transferable   Work/Knowledge Specific

_____

_____

_____

_____

_____

_____

Interests

What do you most enjoy doing? What do you least enjoy? Make some lists.

I enjoy:

_____

_____

_____

_____

_____

_____

I do not enjoy:

_____

_____

_____

_____

_____

_____

Values

What would you most like to have in the work you do? Security, independence, autonomy, being part of a team, challenge, self-expression, financial rewards, recognition, guidance, mentoring, creativity, leadership, diversity, humour, responsibility, self-reliance, dependence, interpersonal relationships, ownership of projects, opportunity to be innovative? *This list is not exclusive.* List the values you would most like to have in the work you do.

Values:

_____

_____

_____

_____

_____

_____

Experiences

List experiences you think will contribute to potential future employment.

Paid Work Experiences:

_____

_____

_____

_____

_____

_____

_____

_____

Volunteer Work Experiences:

_____

_____

_____

_____

_____

_____

_____

_____

Extracurricular Experiences:

_____

_____

_____

_____

_____

_____

_____

Work Environment

What is important to you about your work environment? Size of
organization, location, stability, risk-taking, innovation, flexibility, growth-oriented, easy-going, fast-paced, deadline driven,
formal or informal dress, practical or theoretical, security, competition, indoor or outdoor, work at home or in an office, travel,
cutting edge, well established? This list is not exclusive. List
what you feel is important about your work environment.

The work environment I would prefer includes:

_____

_____

_____

_____

_____

_____

_____

_____

_____

Career Areas and Types of Work

Make a list of possible areas of interest.

Types of work that interest me include:

_____

_____

_____

_____

_____

_____

EXPLORING WORK OPPORTUNITIES

You have lists of your *skills, interests, values, experiences* and *preferred environments, along with areas of potential interest.* The challenge is to match those lists with possible work opportunities. While conducting your research, look for career areas and organizations/industries where your skills and experiences best fit. Remember, most organizations, regardless of their primary focus, hire people for all areas of their business, including their human resources, advertising, public relations, marketing, sales, finance, legal, purchasing, physical plant, and other departments. So do not rule out any possibility without exploring it completely.

Why Do Research?

- Learning all you can about a career area, an organization and/or an individual is essential in targeting your résumé and preparing for information and employment interviews
- Through research, you can broaden your areas of potential interest and skills fit
- The research process allows you to begin to develop the network that will be helpful later on in your search for work
- Conducting research exposes you to a particular industry's unique terminology or jargon
- While carrying out your research you will begin to gain a better understanding of the world of work and the particular area in which you have an interest
- Researching provides a structure to the process of looking for work
- Research helps you relate your skills and experiences to specific work opportunities

Potential Stumbling Blocks to Conducting Effective Research

- Do not understand the importance of conducting research
- Do not know where to start
- Do not know where to begin to look for information
- Do not allow enough time for research
- Do not give research a high enough priority in the process of looking for work
- Feel shy about calling strangers and asking them for an information interview
- Have not clearly identified skills and therefore do not know where to look for a fit

This chapter will help you overcome these blocks.

Sources of Information

Libraries

As you know, effective research takes time - allocate an adequate amount. There will never be a more appropriate investment in your future. A college or university career resource centre or library, is an excellent place to begin your research. Public libraries have fairly extensive career and employment information sections. In any library, be sure to ask for help if you need it. For instance, as a start, ask where the following resources are:

- Directories of occupations, such as the National Occupation Classification

- Industry specific directories

- Association directories

- Career profiles and monographs

- Alumni profiles, if your college or university career resource library has them

- Books, magazines and newspaper articles on your career area of interest

- Salary information

- Industry outlooks and trends

- Company profiles

- Annual reports

- Graduate surveys - if your college or university career resource library has them

- Market surveys - where employers in certain areas have been surveyed

- Career talks - most likely found in your college or university career resource library

- Sample job binders - again, check your career resource library

In each source, look for information on how your skills, interests, values, experiences and preferred environments might match the career area you are researching. Discover information on hiring trends, salaries, duties and responsibilities, skills required, working conditions, environment, career paths and potential advancement, gaining entrance to the field, paying dues, the positives and negatives, backgrounds of the people in the organization, which colleges or universities they attended and where the field is headed. Read everything you can on the career area in which you have an interest. Your objective is to attain as much information as possible.

Researching Specific Industries/Organizations

The following examples of directories are just a sampling from the University of Toronto Career Centre's Resource Library. The list is not intended to be exclusive, but rather to give you an idea of the directories available to you.

> *Canadian Key Business Directory*
>
> *The Blue Book of Canadian Business*
>
> *Scott's Industrial Directories*
>
> *Dunn's Regional Directory of Service Companies*
>
> *Million Dollar Directory*
>
> *Aviation & Aerospace Directory of Canada*
>
> *Canadian Publishers' Directory*
>
> *Directory of Associations in Canada*
>
> *Directory of Canadian Employment Agencies*
>
> *Science and Engineering Employment Directory for Canada*
>
> *The Official Directory of Canadian Museums and Related Institutions*
>
> *Bowen's Media Directory*
>
> *Broadcaster Spring Directory*
>
> *Directory of Community Services*
>
> *Directory of Canadian Architects*
>
> *Directory of Management Consultants*
>
> *Standard and Poors' Register*

Directory of Labour Organizations in Canada

Directory of Canadian Marketing Research Organizations

Directory of Computer Services

World Directory of Environmental Organizations

Boss Directory of Canadian Surveyors & Mapping

Boss Directory of Canadian Construction Companies

Directory of Canadian Companies Overseas

I.T. Top Shops, Leading Canadian Users of Information Technology

Canadian Biotechnology Company Directory

Directory of Manufacturers

Non-Profit Organizations Directory

Ward's Business Directory of U.S. Private and Public Companies

Canadian Forest Industries Directory

Advertising Career Directory

Thomas Register of American Manufacturers

Electronic Information Sources

Most public libraries offer access to information sources through CD-ROM products and on-line database search services. Individual companies can also be sourced through these services. Up-to-date information would include directory data, article citations and financial reports.

Examples include:

CBAC (Canadian Business and Current Affairs): Indexes articles from more than 200 periodicals, 300 magazines and 10 newspapers

Compact D/Canada (Disclosure): Financial information on more than 7,000 major Canadian public companies, privately held federally registered companies, federal and provincial Crown corporations

Canadian Business Disk: Full-text articles from newspapers published by Southam, including the *Toronto Star* and the *Ottawa Citizen*

Moody's Corporate and International Company Data: Contains financial information on more than 470 Canadian companies and 17,000 U.S. and international corporations

ABI/INFORM: Taken from more than 800 publications; abstracts from articles containing information on companies, products, business trends, management policies and techniques

Business Periodicals Ondisc: The full text of articles from more than 300 journals indexed on ABI/INFORM

Microlog: Index of more than 80,000 titles; included are Canadian research reports, parliamentary committee reports, government documents and scientific and technical reports

Moody's Manuals: Include brief corporate history, business and products, list of subsidiaries and properties, officers and financial reports

Standard and Poor's Corporation Records

Disclosure Corporate Snapshots: Source of financial information about public corporations

Annual Reports

Annual reports provide answers to crucial questions you might have. For example: What does the company do? What are its products or services? What has its financial performance been? What are its future plans? Annual reports are multipurpose documents that disclose information about an organization's earnings, financial resources, actions and objectives. Technological advances, new products and acquisitions are highlighted.

One important question you will need to answer is whether or not this specific company is a subsidiary or a division of a larger organization. Sources for answers to this question may be found in both annual reports and in literature supplied by the organization to career and employment centres.

Company Rank

Magazines and newspapers produce publications such as:

> *Report on Business Magazine: The Top One Thousand Companies*
> *Fortune 500: The Largest U.S. Industrial Corporations*
> *Canadian Business 500*
> *Financial Post 500: Canada's Largest Corporations*
> *The Corporate 1000*
> *Canada's 100 Fastest Growing Companies*

Small Business

The most effective means of gathering information about smaller organizations is often to talk to people in the organization itself. However, before doing so, check regional directories, chambers of commerce, small business associations, boards of trade and better business bureaus, as well as newspapers and magazines for information.

Government Publications

All levels of government: federal, provincial and municipal -- produce literature and often directories. The literature would outline the various departments within the government and their primary focus. Directories list the names and telephone numbers of key individuals and departments. The telephone book also lists federal and provincial numbers for ministries and departments. Examples of government publications include:

> *Women in the Federal Public Service of Canada: A Decade of Change*
> *Directory of Offices - Federal*
> *KWIC Index to Services - Annual*
> *Put Yourself in the Picture: A Guide to Local Government*
> *Government of Canada Telephone Directory*
> *Provincial Governments' Telephone Directories*

> *The Government Relations Handbook - Federal*
> *Hot 100: A Quick Guide to Federal Programs and Services for Youth*
> *Guide to Federal Programs and Services*

Career Days/Career Fairs

Career fairs, normally organized by your college or university employment centre or professional associations, provide you with the opportunity to gain information about organizations and industries and allow for an initial contact.

Association Memberships

Belonging to an association that represents the field in which you are interested provides you with invaluable networking opportunities as well as access to their newsletters and publications.

Alumni Associations

Getting involved in your college or university alumni association is another source for networking and attaining information on work opportunities.

INFORMATION INTERVIEWING

"Information interviewing" is a term used frequently by career and employment counsellors. It simply means going out and talking to people to gather information on the work in which you have an interest.

Developing a List of People You Would Like to Interview

- Check with your career services centre to see if they have a list of people who have agreed to be interviewed by students or recent graduates

- Ask all the people you know if they can give you the name of individuals doing the type of work in which you are interested
- Contact your co-op supervisors, sponsors and all former employers
- Talk to friends, neighbours, parents' friends, relatives, professors
- Look through association membership lists.
- Find the names of people through directories, newspaper articles, trade journals
- Use every opportunity -- at a party, in a class or at the cottage -- to let people know that you are looking for people to talk to in order to gather information in a particular field.

Preparation for an Information Interview

Develop questions such as:

- What skills are required for entrance to this field?
- What is the academic background most sought?
- How did you get started in this type of work?
- What are the typical entry-level positions?
- What do you like most about the work you do?
- What are some of the frustrations?
- If you had it to do over, would you have done anything differently?
- What training or education have you needed since you started?
- What might a typical day's activities be?
- What changes do you see in the future?
- Is this a growth area?
- Which associations do you belong to? Do they have student memberships?
- Is there a typical career path in this area?
- Are there other people you think it might be helpful for me to speak to?
- How are positions filled?
- Is there any advice you wish you had been given when you were starting out?

Practice asking these questions with a friend or relative.

Contact someone you know to do the first real interview.

Research the organization for which the person you are going to interview works.

Find out as much as you can about the field.

Call to Make the Arrangements

- Introduce yourself and explain that you are in the process of conducting research to gather career information: "Good morning, my name is Ann Wong. I am a student at ABC College and I am doing research on careers in the area of_____. I have done a fair amount of library work and now feel that I would really benefit from being able to talk to someone in the field. I wondered if you might be able to spare 20 minutes of your time for me to come to your office to talk to you? If someone referred you, mention it."
- If the individual agrees, arrange a mutually convenient time and get specific directions to the place of work. If you are unsure where it is, do a practice visit ahead of time.
- If the person says no, ask if she/he can suggest anyone else who might be willing to talk to you. Be sure to thank the person for any suggestions and for the time spent with you on the phone.
- Be on time for the interview!
- Dress as you would for an employment interview -- you want to leave a positive impression, as you do not know when your paths may cross again.
- Do not stay beyond the agreed upon time.
- Always be friendly and polite.
- Be sure to thank the person when you leave, and also write a thank you note for taking the time to meet with you.

Information interviewing is an invaluable source of career and work information. It affords you the advantage of seeing the workplace, talking to an experienced individual, learning how someone enters the field, hearing about the advantages and disadvantages, and receiving advice on how you might proceed.

It takes courage to arrange your first information interview, particularly if you are somewhat shy. Just remember, the results are worth every ounce of courage it takes.

The Value of Volunteering

In the past, volunteering meant giving of your free time to help a cause in which you believed. It still means that, but with an added '90s twist. Volunteering is now used to gain experience, to develop new skills and to see first-hand, what a particular environment is like. Perhaps you have gathered information on the types of work you think you might want to do, but are either not ready or have been unable to find paid work. Offering your time as a volunteer is a worthwhile thing to do. There is potential volunteer work available in every organization, whether it is in social services or the computer field. Check with your career/employment centre to see if it lists volunteer opportunities. If it does not, or does not have the type of opportunity you would like, approach organizations on your own and ask if you would be able to volunteer some time with them. Treat the approach the way you would a paid work opportunity.

Applying for Volunteer Work

- Call to make an appointment
- Research the organization
- Develop questions you would like to ask
- Take a copy of your résumé
- Dress appropriately
- Clearly articulate the amount of time you have to offer
- Take your commitment seriously

Putting It All Together

Assuming you took advantage of all the information in this chapter so far, what would you have done? Presumably you would have done extensive library research, volunteered your time in order to see first-hand what the work entails and conducted a number of information interviews. Now is the time to see what you have learned from your research. What work opportunities match your skills and experiences?

Complete the following exercise when you have concluded your research.

List the types of work you would like to do:

_____

_____

_____

_____

_____

_____

List the skills required for the type of work and place a check mark beside the skills you have:

_____   _____

_____   _____

_____   _____

_____   _____

_____   _____

_____   _____

_____   _____

_____   _____

_____   _____

List the skills you will have to develop:

_____

_____

_____

_____

_____

_____

_____

_____

You now have a good idea of (a) the type of work you would like to do; (b) the skills required for the work; (c) the skills you already have; and d) the skills you will need to acquire.

Next Steps

If you are still in school you have the advantage of preparing for the type of work you want to do. Here are some of the things you might consider:

- Try to get a summer job or part-time work
- Volunteer your time in the area in which you have an interest
- Continue to learn all you can about the area
- Participate in the Extern program if your college or university has one
- Take full advantage of all co-op programs available to you
- Take courses to help you develop the skills you are missing
- Begin to develop your network of people who work in the area

If you are graduating, have recently graduated or already have full-time work experience, you will want to follow your research by:

- Registering with your college or university career/employment service
- Beginning to develop a network of people involved in the field
- Getting out and talking to possible employers
- Beginning to respond to employment advertisements
- Researching the individual organizations in which you have an interest
- Developing a marketing plan

Your next step will be to develop a marketing plan. Don't know how? See the next chapter!

Chapter 4

MARKETING YOURSELF

INTRODUCTION

All organizations live or die by their marketing plans. They may have the most innovative and useful product imaginable, but if no one knows about it, it will not sell. Can you imagine Microsoft, despite the brilliance of its creator and the user-friendly nature of its product, selling the millions and millions of copies it has without an effective marketing plan? No!

Well, the same theory holds for people looking for work. Unless you and your talents are effectively introduced to potential employers, you will have difficulty selling yourself as a future employee.

You will have the edge in finding work if you have a clear idea of:

- The product - you
- The market - potential employers
- Sources of employment - where to look
- Strategies for self marketing - a good résumé and a good approach
- Presentation - well developed interview skills
- Balance - the ability to pace yourself while looking for work

DEVELOPING A MARKETING PLAN

Developing your first personal marketing plan may be a challenge, but learning how to develop a marketing plan is a skill you will be able to use throughout your working life. A marketing plan provides a structure to what might otherwise seem a daunting task. It will help you focus on your skills and experiences while you map out a strategy you can follow throughout the period of looking for work.

MARKETING PLAN: PHASE ONE

The Product

The product, as you know, is you. Complete the following exercise:

What skills am I selling?

Personal	Transferable	Work/Knowledge Specific
_____	_____	_____
_____	_____	_____
_____	_____	_____
_____	_____	_____
_____	_____	_____
_____	_____	_____
_____	_____	_____

What experiences do I want to highlight?

_____

_____

_____

_____

_____

_____

In which areas and/or organizations am I most interested?

_____

_____

_____

_____

_____

_____

_____

MARKETING PLAN: PHASE TWO

The Market

The next source of information comes from the research you have conducted. Understanding the market is an invaluable skill to develop, as the world of work will continue to change at a rapid pace. Learning what those changes are and how to capitalize on them will set you apart from your competition, both when you are employed and during periods of looking for work. Understanding the major factors that affect change will open doors to future employment for you.

CURRENT TRENDS

Jobs are disappearing and being replaced by work that needs to be accomplished. This work may take the form of continuing employment, or it may be contract, part-time, temporary or project. According to a survey by Murray Axmith & Associates, 87% of the 1,034 responding firms indicated they can no longer offer job security.[5] Rather than being depressing news, this new factor in employment can be an opportunity for you to have more flexibility, diversity and balance in your life than the traditional job offered. Learn how to make today's market work for you.

In an article in *Fortune* magazine, Thomas A. Stewart writes, "We spend our days on projects: designing a new jetliner, launching a product, preparing a lawsuit, re-engineering the billing process. Projects are conceived, staffed up, completed and shut down." He then quotes Warren Bennis of the University of California as saying, "This kind of work leads to adaptive, rapidly changing temporary systems...task forces composed of groups of relative strangers with diverse professional backgrounds and skills organized around problems to be solved."[6]

To market yourself for this workplace, you must understand what employers want and need, continually upgrade your skills and be in the right place at the right time with the right skills and the right method of marketing your skills. It also involves being aware of market trends and the areas where growth is being predicted. Current areas of growth include: technology, environment, health care, training and international opportunities.

Why are these areas seen as growth industries? Everyone is aware of the speed with which technology is advancing. Our everyday life is affected by technological change. The number of homes with computers, access to Internet, microwaves, cellular phones, compact disks, voice mail and satellite disks is growing daily. It takes people with many skills, from the designers to the manufacturers to the marketing and sales staff to the advertisers to the finance people and many, many others, to keep up with evolving technology. There are thousands of work opportunities as a result of technology.

Our planet is suffering from too many years of neglect. Governments around the world are turning their attention to the decay through legislation and R & D efforts. Work opportunities are being created daily for people with the skills to address the world's environmental issues. These opportunities are not reserved for scientists, environmental engineers and policy makers alone.

The population is aging. The huge cohort of baby boomers has reached middle age, and along with that dubious honour is beginning to experience all the issues of aging. Health care, the design of health products, the provision of home care and the discovery of new medications are but a few of the potential areas of emerging work opportunities. These opportunities are not limited to doctors, nurses, scientists, physiotherapists, occupational therapists, pharmacists, engineers, home care workers and social workers. Reaching middle age also brings with it increased income, the ability to travel, to buy cottages and so forth. There are many opportunities being created by demographic changes

Lifelong learning is now being accepted as an integral part of participation in today's workplace. The need for new skills and skills sets has reached a level never seen before. Governments and private corporations are acknowledging this need with financial commitments, which in the past were only paid lip service. For the country and a company to stay competitive, ongoing training is essential. Work opportunities will be available to people with the technical skills required, as well to people with strong teaching and training skills.

International work opportunities abound. As borders shrink and the world becomes linked through technological advances, individuals with experience living in different countries and cultures, who are able to speak a number of languages and who have skills required in the global market will be sought after. Whether your experience is in development, finance, law, teaching, medicine, nursing, business or the environment, more international opportunities are becoming available.

The trends mentioned above are just some of the areas where work opportunities exist. The key is in understanding what is happening in the market and knowing how to take advantage of it.

MARKETING PLAN: PHASE THREE

Sources of Employment Opportunities

This phase of your marketing plan is going to take you beyond the research stage and into actualizing your search for employment. It involves understanding the sources of employment and developing an effective network.

Newspapers

Both daily and business newspapers have classified sections in which employers list positions. These are important sources of available work, and also give a good sense of the industries that are hiring and the types of qualifications being sought.

Trade and Professional Journals

Trade and professional journals often include an employment section, which again is worth perusing both for openings and to get a sense of what is available and what skills are being sought.

Government Publications

Many provincial governments have publications that list employment opportunities. Although financial restraint has considerably limited government positions, there is still hiring being done, often through these publications.

Canada Employment Centres

Anyone eligible to work in Canada is free to register with the local Canada Employment Centre, where thousands of jobs are listed. Although many of these positions are not suitable for individuals with college or university education, the Canada Employment Centres often do include positions where skills may be learned and enhanced.

Employment Agencies or Third Party Agencies

Employment agencies or third party agencies are private licensed organizations that work to find a fit between an individual and an employer's needs. There are very professional firms and those whose ethics are not of as high a caliber. If you plan to use such agencies, research their credibility before signing anything and be aware that the fee should always be paid by the employer, not you. There are also consulting firms that specialize in a particular field, for example computer science.

Networking

"Networking" is a term frequently used by professionals in the career development field and perhaps misunderstood by those outside it. Networking simply means getting out and talking to everyone you can think of who might be helpful in your search for work. It involves making as many contacts as possible and effectively taking advantage of the connections you make. Networking helps you in your research, increases your self-esteem and might give you leads on available positions.

A preliminary networking list would include: family, friends, neighbours, professors, coaches, classmates, former supervisors from both paid and volunteer work, people you have met through clubs and activities, professional groups, alumni, contacts met at parties, events or receptions, as well as employers you met at career days.

Before you contact people in your network, do your homework - know what your skills and experiences are, the type of work in which you are interested and something about the field and/or organization in which you would like to work. Be prepared to give your contacts copies of your résumé, so they might pass them on to people they know, thus expanding your network. Follow up with the people with whom you have talked, remind them that you are still looking and appreciate their interest and assistance. Remember - networking works both ways. By accepting help, you are offering your own when it is needed. Networking works - make a commitment to it!

Do's and Don't's of Networking at a Party
(from *Making Contact*, Barry Siskind)

Do give everyone individual attention

Do develop superior listening skills

Do act professionally

Do stay mobile

Do maintain eye contact

Do keep your promises

Don't look over someone's shoulder when speaking to them

Don't try to impress people by being something you are not

Don't smoke or consume excessive alcohol

Don't drop names

Don't complain

Volunteer Work

Volunteering is an important way to gather information and can lead to many positions. Through your volunteer work you learn about an organization and its environment, and you also have the opportunity of proving yourself and demonstrating your skills. Remember the old adage about being in the right place at the right time - volunteering often accomplishes just that! It is important to keep in mind that you *are* proving yourself. Even though you are not being paid, it is important to be responsible, reliable, mature and committed.

The Internet

The Internet is the latest source of employment leads to emerge. Internet resources are being added daily. There are thousands of electronic bulletin board systems and a growing number of information services. Most students have access to the Internet through their college or university. Employment-related resources are extensive and well worth investigating. Surfing the Information Highway can be fun and a worthwhile source of employment opportunities. However, it can also be extremely time-consuming. Keep your surfing in balance with the rest of your investigative work.

MARKETING PLAN: PHASE FOUR

Develop Your Strategies for Finding Work

Establish your time frame

- Are you going to be working on finding work full-time or part-time?
- How much time do you plan to set aside each day or each week for your search?
- How long do you think looking for work is going to take?
- What is the average length of time for someone with your education, skills and experience?

Do a quick review of your research done in chapter 2

- Did you make a list of the type of work you might be interested in doing?
- Did you make a list of organizations that interested you?
- Have you done all the research you can on the industry or organization?
- Do you have a broad network of contacts?
- Are you aware of the skills wanted by employers in your field of interest?
- Do your skills and experiences match?

Finalize the list of organizations you plan to target

- After reviewing the list you have made, prioritize it. Decide which organizations you want to approach first.
- Determine your method of approach. The method is dependent on a number of variables. If you are responding to an advertisement, it will tell you how to apply, whether it be by résumé and covering letter, by phone or in person. If you are making speculative inquiries, determine which method is most comfortable for you.

Develop your network

- Make a list of people you think might be helpful to you as you look for work. Include family, friends, parents' friends, neighbours, professors, former employers, coaches, teachers, volunteer supervisors and anyone else you think might be helpful.
- Contact all these people and ask them for their assistance. Tell them the type of work you would like to do and the organizations in which you are interested. Give them a copy of your résumé and ask them to give it to anyone they think might have an opening in the areas you have outlined.
- Begin to write covering letters to the organizations you have researched.
- Attend conferences and seminars in your field with the intention of meeting and talking to people who might know of openings.
- Volunteer with organizations in which you have an interest.
- Become extremely knowledgeable about the area in which you are interested.

Small Business

If you are interested in working for a small business, your approach will be different than it might be with a larger organization. You will need to make personal contact with the owner(s) to research the business and to explore the possibility of work opportunities. Small businesses seldom advertise openings in traditional sources. Their positions are much more likely to be filled through word of mouth. If you are interested in working for a small business, networking is essential. Another approach to small business may be volunteering. This would give you a chance to assess the workplace, and it would give the employer the opportunity to get to know you and your abilities. Most first interviews for positions in small businesses take place on the phone, so be prepared.

To explore small businesses in your area, consult the local chamber of commerce, board of trade, professional associations, small business associations, trade publications and - network, network, network!

Marketing Plan: Phase Five

Presentation

Before we begin to talk about interview skills, we need to be sure you truly understand how to make the match between your skills and experience and the skills being sought by potential employers. Complete the following chart. If you have difficulty, go back and review chapters 2 and 3.

Linking Your Skills and Experience to an Employer's Requirements

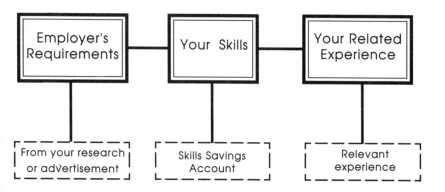

INTRODUCTION TO INTERVIEWING

To pretend that going for an interview is easy would be unfair. Most people are somewhat intimidated by the thought of an interview. There are a number of potential explanations for this. First, by the time people looking for work receive an invitation to an interview, they have often received a number of rejection letters. Their self-esteem, pride, confidence in what they have to offer, to say nothing of rent, food and clothing may be at stake. Second, with the exception of extreme extroverts, most of us find having to sell ourselves to strangers somewhat unnerving. Third, and perhaps most important, interview skills are not innate, they must be developed.

This part of the chapter will address each of these issues and provide advice on eliminating them as obstacles. The focus, however, will be on the final point - interview skills must be developed and practised. There are very tangible ways to learn how to be an effective interviewee, how to prepare for interviews, how to evaluate your performance and how to improve on it. After you study the information in this chapter, you will be prepared to tackle head-on the challenges of interviews and make them work for you.

Effective Interviews

Learning to be an effective interviewee in today's workplace is as important as having a powerful résumé and covering letter. Change is the operative word as we approach the twenty-first century, and it is equally applicable to the work world. Inherent in this reality is the fact that you will have to be prepared to be interviewed each time you change the work you are doing. Developing strong interview skills is a key ingredient in your career success.

What is the point of an interview from an employer's perspective?

- To meet the person who sent the résumé
- To further explore a possible fit between what the interviewee has to offer and the work in question
- To assess the candidate's qualifications and potential
- To explore the interviewee's ability to think quickly
- To assess presentation style, command of the language and knowledge of the field
- To determine the candidate's understanding of the position and organization
- To compare this applicant with others who are being interviewed

What do you - the applicant - want to accomplish in the interview?

- To present yourself in the most positive light
- To convince the employer of the strong fit between your skills and qualifications and the position
- To demonstrate your understanding of the position and the organization
- To articulate effectively what skills you have to offer, how your skills have been developed and where they have been used
- To find out more about the position and the organization
- To determine whether you would actually want to do the work if it is offered
- To decide if the organization is one for which you would want to work
- To conclude whether or not the position is one that would lead you in the direction you would like to go with your career

DIFFERENT TYPES OF INTERVIEWS

Single Interviewer

One person conducts this type of interview. It is the most common interview situation. The interview may take place at a career or employment service centre on campus or in the interviewer's office. The interviewer is normally either a human resource officer or a manager in the department in which the work is located.

Group Interview

Group interviews may be conducted by anywhere from two to twelve interviewers. Frequently the team consists of a representative from the human resource department, the manager of the department, the person to whom you would report and possibly, a potential co-worker. The group members will have decided ahead of time on the questions they want asked and who will ask them.

Behavioural Interview

This interview focuses on how you would react in various situations. The situations are chosen from potential real examples of issues facing the particular organization. The goal in behavioural interviews is to determine how well the candidate is able to think quickly, relate experience to situation and solve problems.

Subsequent Interviews

More often than not, there is more than one interview before an offer is made. A second and sometimes third or fourth interview is conducted to determine how effective a fit the position is with the person being interviewed. Often subsequent interviews are conducted by more senior people or by people who are direct supervisors. Tours of the organization and/or lunch or dinner are frequently part of subsequent interviews. If you are invited to the employer's location be sure to observe the environment while you are there and try to get answers to the following questions: Do people look happy? Do they appear to be enjoying their work? Is the atmosphere relaxed? Is it an environment in which you would be comfortable?

Telephone Interviews

More and more these days, employers, in an effort to save time, conduct initial interviews on the telephone. Preparing for a telephone interview is no different from preparing for an in-person interview. However, there is a significant difference in the interview itself, in that you only have the interviewer's tone of voice to measure responses to your answers, rather than expressions on the face. Telephone interviews are a challenge for people who are not particularly comfortable on the phone. The key for such people would be to practise their telephone skills before the interview. An advantage to telephone interviews is that you may look at notes, your résumé, project work or any other material you feel would be of assistance.

COMPONENTS OF AN INTERVIEW

Introductions

Most interviewers begin an interview by trying to make you, the interviewee, feel at ease. They may initiate conversation by asking whether you had any trouble finding the office, commenting on the parking or lack of it, mentioning the weather or some other neutral topic. This period gives you a chance to calm down, gather your thoughts and focus on the interview itself.

First Stage of the Interview

After the ice-breaking period, the interviewer may elaborate on the position for which you are being interviewed and then ask you what interests you about the position. This is normally followed by general questions about your skills and experiences. Examples of such questions might be:

- Tell me about yourself.
- Can you give me an idea of why you chose your particular area of study?
- What would you say were your strongest skills?
- Tell me about an accomplishment about which you feel particularly proud.
- What kind of boss do you prefer and why?
- What did you enjoy most about your last job?
- What did you enjoy least and why?
- What would you consider an area of weakness?
- Do you prefer to work alone or as part of a team?
- You mentioned that you had strong organizational skills, can you give me an example of a work setting, where you would have used those skills?
- What skills have you developed in your past two jobs?
- Your experience appears to be primarily in the area of public relations, how would you transfer that experience to this environment?

Second Stage of the Interview

The interviewer now has a sense of who you are and what your skills are. It is time to move to more specific questions directly related to the position for which you are being interviewed. At this stage of the interview, the interviewer wants to determine as definitely as possible, whether you can do the job and how much of a contribution you would make. If the position is a technical one, you can expect to be asked detailed technical questions. If the position is in an area where there is a specific body of knowledge, the questions asked will address that knowledge.

Examples might include the following kinds of questions:

- What effect do you think the EU has had and will have on our business?
- Why is the density of the concrete important?
- What sources would you use to research this issue?
- What contacts would you start with to build your clientele?
- What aspect of SAS is most important to the research we are doing?
- How might you present our research findings to senior administration?
- How long would it take you to write a 5,000 word article?
- What type of design do you think would be best suited to this project?

Third Stage of the Interview

It is now your turn to demonstrate your understanding of the position and the organization by asking the questions you have both prepared ahead of time and thought of during the interview. Relate the questions to specific aspects of the position. You will also want to use this period to clarify any issues you feel are unclear. General questions you might want to ask are:

- How would success in this position be defined?
- Can you tell me more about the training program and who has access to it?
- Who do you see as your major competition?
- Is the senior administration committed to innovation?
- What might be the potential career paths for someone in this position?
- What do you anticipate the largest challenges facing the company to be?

- How committed is the company to the community and how is this played out?
- Your annual report indicates a significant decrease in the amount of research you are conducting. Do you perceive this to be an ongoing trend?

Final Stage of an Interview

The final stage of an interview allows the interviewer to tell the interviewee when the hiring decision will be made, expected starting time, salary range, if it has not already been discussed, and any other details related to the position. It is also an opportunity for you to ask any questions you still might have.

The interview normally ends with handshakes and the promise to be in touch when a decision has been made.

When You Have an Interview

The preparation done before an interview is often as important as your performance during the interview. In preparing for an interview, keep the following tips in mind:

- Review your skills, experience and accomplishments. Go back to Chapter 1. Consider how the skills you outlined relate to the position for which you are being interviewed. Think about which skills and experiences you want to highlight in the interview.
- Review the research you did on the position and the organization. Re-read the annual report, company literature and newspaper and magazine articles. Talk to contacts who are more familiar with the organization. You should be clear on the nature of the organization's work, where it stands in comparison to others in the field, what services or products it highlights, new initiatives and size. What are its mission and strategic plans? Are there organizational changes scheduled? What is the outlook for the industry in which it operates?
- Re-read the advertisement, if there was one. Study the

qualifications required, primary duties and any other factor mentioned in the ad such as location, travel and/or salary.

- Know the interviewer's name(s). Find out who will be interviewing you. Will it be one person or more than one? Ask for names and position titles.

- Bring extra copies of your résumé. There may be someone at the interview who does not have a copy of your resume or the interviewer may refer to a section of the resume and you may want to follow on your own copy.

- Be friendly to everyone you meet. You have no idea who has input into the hiring decision, so cover all bases. Secretaries and receptionists often have much more influence than you might think.

- Go to the site ahead of time to make sure you are comfortable with how to get there. Visiting the site ahead of time will also reduce your anxiety considerably.

Tips on things *not* to do in the interview:

- Do not criticize former employers, co-workers or professors.
- Do not ask about salary or benefits until the recruiter raises the issue, or ask at the end of the interview.
- Do not chew gum or eat candy.
- Do not underdress or overdress for the interview. Before the interview, ask about the organization's dress code.
- Do not wear excessive jewelry or perfume.
- Do not avoid eye contact with anyone during the interview.

Following the Interview

After every interview, review how you did. If there were questions with which you had difficulty, re-think your answers for the next time. Excellence in interviewing comes as a result of practice. Congratulate yourself on the positive aspects of your performance.

Write a thank-you letter to the interviewer. The letter may be short. Thank the person for his or her time and restate your interest in the position. It is also an opportunity for you to briefly clarify a point you feel was missed.

Follow-up

If you have not heard from the employers by the date the interviewer gave you in the interview, call them. Politely inquire if they have made a decision. If they have, they may tell you on the spot, so be prepared for whichever result. If they have decided to hire someone else - thank them for the opportunity of the interview and tell them that you enjoyed meeting them. You never know when your paths may cross again. You might want to ask the interviewer for feedback, which you could use in future applications. Most interviewers are pleased to provide feedback.

Last Thoughts on Interviewing

You will get better with every interview you have. Interviewing is a skill, and like all skills, it can be improved with practice. And remember - assess your skills and do your research. Success will be yours!

Sample Record-Keeping Sheet

Organization - ABC Consulting

Action	Date	Follow up done
Telephone call	April 23	
Letter & Résumé sent	April 24	May 8
Appointment		
1st Interview	May 15	

Letter of Rejection	June 14	On to the next!!!
2nd Interview		
Offer Made		
Offer Accepted		

Have a separate sheet for each organization you contact. You might want to keep your record-keeping sheets in a **marketing plan binder** divided by organization. This is a good way to keep all correspondence, notes or copies of covering letters pertaining to a particular organization together for easy reference.

At the front of your marketing plan binder, place **weekly report sheets.**

Weekly Report Sheet

Week of: _____

____ Letters written
____ Letters & résumés sent
____ Applications completed
____ Telephone calls made
____ Information interviews
____ Contacts established
____ Invitations to interviews
____ Follow-up calls made

HOW TO FEEL GOOD WHILE LOOKING FOR WORK

Looking for work can be a strain on your normally healthy self-esteem. It is sometimes difficult to accept that not every employer you approach wants to interview you, that some never return your phone calls or respond to your letters, that once granted an interview you are not offered the job.

Rejection during a looking-for-work period is part and parcel of the process for 99.9% of people, regardless of the strength of their skills, breadth of experience or degree of self-confidence. Very few people escape the rejection bug.

Okay, so if rejection is an integral component of looking for work, how is it best handled? First, simply acknowledge that you are not the first, nor will you be the last person to feel down or rejected. Second, have a well thought out marketing plan, which builds in a time frame for looking for work. This will provide both structure and incentive. Third, ensure that your plan includes time just for you -- time to relax, to exercise, to be with supportive family and friends, to recharge your looking for work batteries.

Always keep in the forefront of your mind that as a college or university graduate, you have a rich supply of skills and experiences to offer an employer. Furthermore, you will make a valuable contribution to the organization that is wise enough to hire you.

Marketing Plan: Phase Six

Handling an Offer

The offer may be delivered either by phone or by mail, although most frequently it is by phone. If you are absolutely sure that you want the position and you know that details such as salary, location and benefits are acceptable to you, accept on the spot.

If you have not completed all your interviews or have some doubts about the fit of the position, you may wish to ask the interviewer if you could have some time to think it over. Most employers understand a request for time to consider the offer and will negotiate a deadline.

If you have questions that stand in your way of accepting, now is the time to ask them. Ensure that the employer knows you are still interested in the position.

Questions to Ask Before Accepting an Offer:

- Is there a formal training program?
- What is the probation period?
- How much travelling will be involved?
- What is the salary range for this position?
- How often are salaries reviewed?
- What are the benefits, sick leave and vacation allowances?
- What might a typical career path look like for a position such as this?

Salary Negotiation

Most employers have some flexibility when it comes to the salary they offer a potential employee. There are normally salary ranges within which an employer may select a figure to include in an offer. You might want to ask what the salary range is. If the employer responds by saying that the range is $40,000 to $45,000, your response might be, "that is close to what I was expecting, although I was thinking more in the neighbourhood of $48,000." The employer then has the option of sticking to the stated range, but in all likelihood, will offer you the high end or will meet your figure. As in all negotiations, you have to be prepared to compromise. The final decision will depend on how much you really want the particular position.

Turning Down An Offer

Should you decide to turn down an offer, express your appreciation for their interest in you and tactfully explain why you are unable to accept the offer. You might say something like, "It was a very difficult decision, but I think the other position I was offered better fits my needs at this time." It is often advisable to write a letter after you have turned down an offer, once again explaining why and thanking the employer for the interest in you. You never know when or where you may run into that employer again.

MARKETING PLAN: PHASE SEVEN

Balance

Looking for work can be a very difficult and frustrating activity. If you are like most people who have ever looked for work, there will be times when you begin to think that you might never work again. Of course you will! Staying motivated while you look for work is essential. You want to be putting your best effort into every phone call, appointment and interview. To ensure that you will be able to stay positive, build time off into your marketing plan. Take time to:

- Stay in touch with family and friends, particularly those who are supportive
- Plan an exercise program
- Find a part-time or temporary job, which provides both income and diversion
- Take a course you have always wanted to take
- Join a professional association related to your field
- Do an activity you enjoy
- Just have fun
- Learn to treat rejection letters as part of the process and not a personal rejection

Balance allows you to restore your energy, rebuild your self-confidence and get motivated. Your marketing plan provides the framework within which you look for work. Time for recharging the batteries is as important as making a call to that next contact.

Take time for you - it will pay off!

Chapter 5

MANAGING YOUR CAREER

INTRODUCTION

Congratulations, you have landed the position you wanted! It may be your first post-graduation position or one of several you have had to date. What seemed like an endless process of looking for work is finished for the time being. You are gainfully employed and eager to start this new phase of your life.

As those of you who have been working for a while know, planning for your first day at work is in many ways similar to other first days in your life: first day in kindergarten, first day in high school. You'll feel excitement mixed with some anxiety. Remember looking around and thinking everyone else knew exactly what they were doing and where they were going? Remember wondering if you had dressed appropriately? Who should you talk to? Would people be friendly? Would they be helpful? Where would you have lunch? And would you remember all their names?

You survived those other first days and you will survive this one too!

This book has been written to address some of the common concerns new graduates and those with more experience have upon starting a new position and about managing their career effectively in the new workplace. Topics such as changes in the world of work, getting started, what is expected of new employees, paying your dues, and office politics are included in this chapter - and much more!

This is the first day of the rest of your life and you are about to learn how to make it work for you.

Change, Change and More Change

Transition Skills Are Key

> "To succeed in a competitive global environment we must learn not only to survive this chaos of rapid change, but thrive on chaos."
> - Tom Peters, *Thriving on Chaos*

Change is the operative word in describing work today. In this chapter you'll learn the skills you need to effectively deal with the many transitions you will have to make during your career. These include changes in the form of a new position, new rules and definitions of work, and increased need for self-reliance and balance in life. Starting work in a new organization is just the first transition in what promises to be an unending list.

Many professionals in the field of career development believe work is no longer about having a job - it is about a piece of work needing to be done. For this reason, you will notice the word "job" is never used in this book. Rather, "work" or "position" are used instead. The days of jobs and job titles are being replaced by memberships on work teams and/or project teams.

Developing the ability to meet new challenges in a rapidly changing environment is integral to success in the new workplace.

GETTING STARTED IN A NEW POSITION

You have already met and impressed the person or people from the organization who interviewed and hired you. Your skills, education, work experience and interests appeared to them to fit well with those of the organization. The relationship is off to a good start; it is up to you to maintain the momentum.

Most new positions begin with a period of orientation and perhaps training. This is your opportunity to ask questions, observe and form relationships with your co-workers. Everything is new. Its exciting and challenging. Your employer wants you to succeed and will provide all the appropriate support necessary. However, the ball is in your court.

In addition to work-specific skills, other skills will be called on over the next months. These include: self-motivation, reliability, acceptance of responsibility, initiative, communication, team membership, interpersonal skills, learning, analyzing, organizing, time management, maturity, humour, and strong transition skills.

Your employers will want to see that everything you wrote in your résumé and covering letter, and your responses in the interviews, were valid. They will be looking for the potential they saw at the interview stage. Many positions have probationary periods, which last anywhere from three to six months. During this period your performance is appraised and a decision is made in terms of your immediate future with the organization. Getting hired was just the first step. Proving yourself in those first few months is the next.

The organization, regardless of the industry, has a bottom line. That bottom line may be profit, it may be service excellence, it may be increasing market share, it may be expanding internationally or it may be all of the above. The point is that quite separate from you, it has a goal. Your role, and the role of all the other employees, is to meet or exceed that goal. Very few organizations have room for *stars* among their new recruits. In most organizations, it is through being an effective team member that you will make the largest contribution.

And so, with your skills in hand, your potential just chomping at the bit and a commitment to the team, you are ready to launch this phase of your career.

Top Ten Do's and Don'ts for Settling into a New Job

1. Listen more than you talk. Listen to what more experienced people have to say before you add your opinion. The best impression is created by someone who does not say much. But, when he/she does, people listen.

2. If you complete an assignment, ask for another or suggest one for which you feel you are qualified.

3. Keep references to and experiences about your previous employer to a minimum. (And never during the first few months.)

4. Always meet deadlines.

5. If you do not know an answer or how to complete an assignment, either ask someone or research the answer. There is nothing wrong with admitting that you don't know about something as long as you are willing to find out.

6. Always arrive on time and do not be the first person out the door at the end of the day.

7. Do not be afraid to make a mistake - we all make them. The key is to learn from our mistakes and to not repeat them.

8. Make sure that you completely understand assignments. No one minds being asked questions to ensure understanding.

9. Present solutions for problems and learn to be tactful and discreet.

10. Have a vision. Know where you want to be in eighteen months or in two years time.

WHAT IS EXPECTED OF YOU?

Here are some answers to common questions people have about a new workplace. In most cases, it would be appropriate to ask the person to whom you report, or ask a colleague who has been there longer. It is important to have answers to these questions, so you can begin to balance work and your personal life.

Attitude: Employers want self-starters who are able to see the big picture, understand their role in it and have a mature approach to work. They want people who have self-confidence, who are flexible, take pride in their work and are good team players.

Dress: Appropriate dress for your new environment depends on the industry, and on the organization itself. Look around. If you are unsure what the office dress code is, ask. Sometimes over-dressing is as inappropriate as under-dressing.

Telephone: Ask what the preferred telephone answering response is. When answering your own phone, it's usually best to use first name and surname, for example, "Pat Denlock speaking", not "Pat speaking".

Hours: On the first day, ask what the hours are and what is expected in terms of overtime for a person in your position.

Training: Inquire about in-house training programs, and about arrangements to accommodate the completion of your professional designation.

Sick Days: Find out what the policy is on sick days and what the expected procedure is when calling in sick.

Vacation: Check on the amount of vacation you receive if you do not already know, find out how notification of taking holidays is done.

Benefits: Understand your benefits and attain outside coverage if you do not have disability insurance or all the medical, drug, dental and glasses coverage you wish. Sometimes benefits do not apply to you during your introductory probationary period. Be sure to find out about this, as well as the method of reimbursement for expenses such as dental bills and prescriptions.

Media:	Ask what the policy is concerning talking to the press. If you happen to receive a call directly, inform your immediate supervisor of the call and/or request before responding.
Org. Chart:	Ask to see the organizational chart to get a sense of the organization and where you and your department fit.

MANAGING YOUR RELATIONSHIP WITH YOUR SUPERVISOR

Your relationship with the person to whom you report in your first few years may be one of the most important and at times challenging relationships that you have. It can make or break your working experience. Learning to manage that relationship is a key to successfully adapting to your new workplace.

The person to whom you report is presumably more skilled and experienced than you are, has been with the organization longer, has more contacts, more security, more political awareness than you and, perhaps most importantly, has some control over your future. In other words, she or he is in a position to either assist you in attaining your career goals or, if influenced negatively by your behaviour, put roadblocks in your way. The latter scenario fortunately occurs rarely. Most supervisors will work with you to ensure that both you and the organization succeed.

How can you develop a mutually respectful relationship? Approaching your work positively and with enthusiasm will go a long way to establishing an effective relationship. Demonstrating flexibility, willingness to continue learning and developing your skills, volunteering to take on new assignments, being mature and professional, meeting deadlines, being willing to go the extra step and always displaying a co-operative attitude - these will help you build a relationship.

Your relationship with the person to whom you report is a professional one. He or she is not your buddy or your friend. Your working life should be kept separate from your personal life. It is not advisable to confide in your supervisor about personal issues. Keep the relationship professional.

Unfortunately not all supervisors have the management skills we might wish they did. If you have the misfortune of working with someone who you are unable to respect, try to make the best of the situation, as it will not last forever. The individual will not be your supervisor throughout your career. Your goal is to learn all you can, demonstrate your abilities, contribute to the team and continue to develop your skills. In so doing, you will no doubt move forward and have the opportunity of working with someone else in the near future.

Make a commitment to doing everything you can to maintain a positive relationship with the person to whom you report. It will pay off! When you are functioning at a top level, you will make your supervisor look good as well. Earn your supervisor's trust and respect.

Sexual Harassment

It is unfortunate that a section in a book such as this would have to focus on sexual harassment in the workplace, but experience dictates that all employees should be aware of what is appropriate work behaviour and what is clearly not. In all provinces in Canada, human rights statutes prohibit "sex discrimination" in employment. The Supreme Court of Canada in Janzen v. Platy Enterprises Ltd. (man. 1989), 10 C.H.R.R. D/6227 (S.C.C.) defined conduct that constitutes sexual harassment and is discriminatory as follows: "The forms of prohibited conduct that, in my view are discriminatory run the gambit from overt gender-based activity, such as coerced intercourse to un-solicited physical contact to persistent propositions to more subtle conduct such as gender-based insults and taunting, which may reasonably be perceived to create a negative psychological and emotional work environment."

Most organizations today have sexual harassment policies in place and clearly identified individuals to whom you may go in confidence to discuss your concerns around any harassing behaviour you might experience. Most workplaces today strive to provide fair and equitable work environments free of sexual harassment. However, if you feel that you are the victim of sexual harassment, do not wait - find out who to talk to and act immediately. You have a right to work in an environment that is respectful of you as an individual.

PAYING YOUR DUES

Regardless of the organization or industry, your first few years on the job are ones of learning, of being trained, of enhancing your skills, of applying what you learned in school and previous positions to your current work environment, of paying your dues.

What does paying your dues mean? It means doing what every woman and man who went before you did when they were starting out. It means proving yourself. It means demonstrating that you have what it takes. It may also mean doing work that is not as challenging as you would like, working long hours, travelling to less exciting places than those senior to you travel to, handling less interesting clients, staffing areas in the office you may feel are beneath you and it may mean doing what are sometimes referred to as the "gofer" jobs.

Approaching the issue of paying your dues with a positive attitude will not only make the work easier, but also it will make an impression on those senior to you. You will be seen as someone willing to pitch in where needed, a good team member, someone who understands and is committed to the bottom line and who is not afraid to work hard.

On the other hand, new staff who allow their resentment to show or whose behaviour indicates that they think they are above paying their dues give a loud and clear message to senior administration. All organizations have work that is not exciting or challenging, yet it has to be done. A new employee who is more interested in the limelight than in playing a role on the team is likely to be left behind or simply not required in the future.

Paying your dues is part of launching your career and maintaining it. Remember, it is not a period that lasts forever. Try to approach it positively and take every piece of learning you can from it.

Office Politics

We have all heard the expression "office politics", but what does it really mean? Office politics refers to the unofficial side of the organization - the side that may be known only internally. Components of the unofficial side include knowing the following:

- Who's who
- Who's in and who's out
- Who has the power
- Who has the ear of the decision makers
- Whom to avoid
- Who has a reputation for stealing ideas and claiming them as their own
- Who the whiners and trouble-makers are
- How to get things done in spite of people blocking ideas
- What is the CEO's pet interest
- Who is on the fast track
- Who perpetuates office gossip

Office politics are a fact of life in all organizations. The wisest approach is often to stay out of them. However, if that is not possible, play it smart - learn and understand the power structure, use that knowledge to your advantage, and do not join in with the whiners or trouble-makers. Align yourself with the positive people, the people who enjoy their work and who are committed to the organization's goals.

FINDING A MENTOR

What is a mentor? A mentor is someone in your organization who is more senior than your and who knows you and your work and is willing to act as an adviser, a coach, a teacher and a champion of you and your talents.

Having a mentor is not dissimilar to having a personal coach, wise teacher or guru. As more senior member's of the organization, mentors are more experienced, know the ins and outs, understand the inevitable politics, have more connections, have more access to information, have already made significant contributions, know the potential pitfalls, and remember when they were at your stage of their careers and had the privilege of having had help from their own mentors.

Mentors make enormous differences in careers. In addition to what you can learn from them, they often are able to open career doors that otherwise might remain closed to you.

How do you go about finding a mentor? Well, for the first number of months you keep your eyes and ears open. You begin to form a sense of who is who in the organization: who you can learn the most from; who is most open to your questions; who seems interested in your work; who appears to be most respected; who has decision making power; who is recognized outside the organization in the field; and whose style you believe to be most effective.

Once you have formed your opinion about who you might like to be your mentor, begin to volunteer to work on their work teams or on their projects. Take the opportunity to talk to them informally. Learn what you can about their interests and their accomplishments. Observe their style, their method of approaching problems and solving them. However, do not be obvious about it, and don't be a pest.

Finding a mentor happens when a more senior person is impressed by the quality of your work, your integrity, your talent and your commitment. The senior person will decide to play a mentorship role for you, not the other way around. Your job is to do the best work you can and hope that the person you want to notice does so.

Mentors do not necessarily have to work in the same organization or even in the same field. Relatives, neighbours, friends of parents or parents of friends may play a mentorship role for you if you are open to their coaching and advice.

Mentors can and do make enormous differences in the careers of younger people. Mentorship relationships are formed as a result of two people liking and respecting each other. Keep your eye out for someone from whom you can learn and on whom you can model your professional behaviour. The rest will happen naturally.

YOUR DEGREE OR DIPLOMA IS ONLY THE BEGINNING

Once upon a time, graduation from college or university meant the end of formal education and training. As is true of all fairy tales, that was a long time ago! Today's work world is one where there is an on-going need for education and training. The Information Age has changed all the rules related to work in all occupations. Change in technology, systems, communication and globalization dictates the need for continuous upgrading of skills and the development of new ones.

Life-long learning is no longer a phrase unique to educational institutions - it is a fact of life for all of us. International competition is propelling the rate of change. As the nature of work continues to change, so do the skills necessary to accomplish that work. Further education and training are the only answers.

Take advantage of all in-house training offered to you. Be constantly aware, through reading, talking to those more experienced and assessing the marketplace, of the changes occuring and their effect on your area. Find out about the education/

training available to meet those challenges. Charles Handy, the famous management philosopher, said in an interview, "If workers don't continually develop and update their skills, not only will they be of no use to the organization but, worse, they will be a growing burden to the rest of us." Dick Measelle, world-wide managing partner of Arthur Andersen, is quoted in the same article as saying that training people is the only way to give them security in an insecure world. He says, "People are assets, not expenses".[7]

Learn to accept - in fact to enjoy - the prospect of life-long learning. It ensures that work will not be boring. There will always be new challenges to meet, and you will continue to develop and grow.

TIME MANAGEMENT

What Happens When You Do Not Manage Time Well?

- You fall behind on projects/work
- You waste time
- You fail to meet deadlines
- You risk wasting time on the unimportant, at the expense of the important
- You end up always playing catch-up
- You let supervisors and colleagues down
- You put projects at risk
- You endanger renewal of contracts
- You develop a reputation as someone who cannot be trusted

Helpful Tips on Time Management

- Establish objectives for yourself and set goals

- Make a list of things to do in order of their importance
- Avoid frequent interruptions - close your door if possible
- Striving for perfection with issues that do not require perfection, is a waste of time
- Learn to say no if you are already over-extended
- Divide large projects into smaller, more manageable pieces
- Deal with each piece of paper once and get it off your desk
- Procrastination simply causes problems - do it now!
- Build down-time into your schedule so that you can be proactive and not simply reactive
- Learn how to delegate when appropriate

Time Management Exercise

Purpose: To evaluate your time management skills

Method:

1. In the chart on the following page, list the primary activities in which you engage in a typical week. Try to identify the approximate amount of time you spend on each activity. Record the time spent.

2. Place an H (high) beside the most important activities. Place an M (medium) beside those second in priority. Place an L (low) beside those the lowest priority.

Assess your time management skills by examining the activities you have indicated as the highest, medium and lowest priorities and the amount of time spent doing them. Are you spending more time than you should on low priorities? Are all activities necessary? Are you approaching them in the most effective manner? Where might you save time? Are you achieving your goals? If you were grading your time management skills, what mark would you give yourself?

Activities In a Typical Week	Time Spent and Ratings (H,M,L)
....	....
....	....
....	....
....	....
....	....
....	....
....	....
....	....
....	....
....	....
....	....
....	....
....	....
....	....
....	....
....	....

Key Position-Keeping Skills

Employers look for the following qualities in the employees they hope will be with them for awhile:

- Ability to do the job well
- Initiative
- Dependability
- Reliability
- Efficiency
- Loyalty
- Maturity
- Positivism
- Ability to work well as part of a team
- Generosity
- Responsibility
- Creativity

If you already have these skills, use them effectively and to your advantage. If you are missing one or two, work on developing them. Your longevity with most organizations depends on having and continuing to develop these key skills.

FINANCIAL PLANNING

Financial planning used to be something people did when they were older - when they were married and had children. It involved planning to buy a house, a new car, sending the children to college or university, retirement. Today, financial planning is a priority for everyone, and the need for financial planning begins with your first work position after graduation. To avoid being caught between jobs without any income, you must plan for potential periods of unemployment before they happen. Or plan for opportunities for self-employment.

Although buying a car or travel may be foremost on your mind, learning to plan financially for the future is a skill worth learning - and learning now. There are a number of helpful books on the market to make the task easier. They include:

> *The Wealthy Barber: The Common Sense Guide to Successful Financial Planning.* David Chilton. Toronto, Stoddart Publishing Inc. 1989.
>
> *The Money Coach.* Riley Moynes. Toronto, Copp Clark Longman Ltd. 1994
>
> *The Kitchen Table Money Plan.* Barbara McNeill and Robert Collins. Toronto, Harper Collins Publishers, Ltd. 1992
>
> *Landing On Your Feet.* Mara Brown. Toronto, McGraw-Hill Ryerson. 1992.

Starting Point - Develop Your Plan

The first step in financial planning is to determine your income and expenses. Articulating your income is the easy part. It is basically your salary and any other income you are fortunate enough to have. The sample financial statement below will help you identify your fixed expenses and give you a sense of whether you are overspending or are able to save money. Once the financial statement is completed you will be better able to analyze your spending patterns. The next step is to develop a budget.

"Budget" is not a dirty word - it is a guide to effective financial management. It outlines your financial situation as you want it to be, rather than what it currently is. It builds in a savings plan while ensuring that all your essential expenses are covered.

Your Current Financial Picture

Annual income before taxes $...............
Income from employment $...............
Salary income $...............
Self-employed income $...............
Income from dividends $...............
Income from savings accounts $...............

Income from trusts	$ ....
Other income sources	$ ....
Total income	$ ....

Annual Expenses

Rent or condominium fees	$ ....
Mortgage payments	$ ....
Loan payments (student & personal)	$ ....
Property taxes and insurance	$ ....
Other insurance (life, health, disability)	$ ....
Utilities (heat, light, telephone)	$ ....
Cable	$ ....
Home Repairs and Maintenance	$ ....
Food	$ ....
Clothing and Footwear	$ ....
Medical (dentist, prescriptions, glasses)	$ ....
Haircuts	$ ....
Car expenses (gas, maintenance, insurance)	$ ....
Public transportation	$ ....
Education/training expenses (tuition, books)	$ ....
Purchase/lease (cars, household items)	$ ....
Vacations	$ ....
Entertainment (restaurants, fitness, hobbies)	$ ....
Charitable donations	$ ....
Gifts	$ ....
Annual income tax paid	$ ....
Canada/Quebec Pension Plan payments	$ ....
Unemployment Insurance Contributions	$ ....
RRSP Contributions	$ ....
Total expenses	$ _____
Annual cash flow	$ _____
(Income minus expenses)	

How Are You Doing Financially?

Given the results of the previous exercise, read each statement and check off those that are true for you.

_____ I have a regular savings plan to provide for financial emergencies, major purchases

_____ I have a savings plan for investment purposes

_____ I contribute as much as I can to my RRSP

_____ I pay off my credit cards monthly

_____ I am paying off my student loan and personal loans as quickly as possible.

_____ I am planning for my next vacation.

_____ I have adequate health and disability insurance.

_____ I have a pension plan through work.

_____ I have an up-to-date will.

_____ I have arranged for Power of Attorney should I be incapacitated.

_____ I am saving to buy a house or a condominium.

Are you satisfied with how you are handling your finances? If not, which areas would you like to improve?

Areas for improvement:

_____

_____

_____

_____

_____

Monthly Budget Exercise

It may not be a lot of fun, but this budget exercise will give you a sense of how you spend your money and whether you are able to save. If you think you are not able to save, examine the expense side of your budget with an eye to cutting expenditures.

Financial planning is really just common sense: what goes out cannot exceed what comes in. And, if you want to save, you have to plan to do so. You should build a savings plan right into your budget.

Net monthly income (take home pay) $ _____

Expenses

Rent or condominium fees	$................
Mortgage payments	$................
Student loan payments	$................
Other loan payments	$................
Property taxes and insurance	$................
Insurance (life, health, disability)	$................
Utilities (gas, heat, electricity, telephone, cable)	$................
Home repairs/maintenance	$................
Food	$................
Clothing and Footwear	$................
Medical (dentist, doctor, prescriptions, glasses)	$................
Haircuts	$................
Counsellor, psychologist	$................
Car expenses (gas, maintenance, insurance, license)	$................
Parking	$................
Education/training expenses (tuition, books)	$................
RRSP contribution	$................
Purchase or lease of car	$................
Entertainment (restaurants, bars, fitness club)	$................
Sports equipment	$................
Charitable donations	$................
Gifts	$................
Vacation savings	$................

Monthly Savings	$ ....
Other expenses	$ ....
Total monthly expenses	$ _____

Additional Financial Tips

Pay off debts as soon as possible. Start with credit card debts, as interest rates are extremely high. You must begin to pay back your student loan six months from your last day of full-time study. Talk to your bank about making arrangements to begin paying down your debt.

Live within your means. Debt accumulation can become a noose around your neck. Don't overspend - instead, concentrate on beginning a savings program.

Begin contributing to a RRSP as soon as possible. You can invest in a wide variety of financial vehicles and avoid paying tax on your capital gains. And you can deduct the amount of your contribution from your previous year's income.

Try to build a nest egg to cover living expenses.

BALANCING WORK AND PERSONAL LIFE

"Nobody on their deathbed says, 'I wish I had spent more time at the office.'"
- Stephen Covey, *First Things First*

Work is just one part of your life. There are 168 hours in a week. Approximately 56 are spent sleeping. Therefore there are 112 waking hours in a week. If you worked 40 of those hours, you would be left with 72. Learning to balance your work hours with the remaining 72 waking hours is essential to both your well-being and your career.

The old adage, "all work and no play makes Johnny (or Jane) a dull boy (or girl)," has tremendous truth to it. Your success in life depends on your ability to find a balance. A balance between work and the rest of your life -- your family, friends, interests, sports, fitness, schooling, training and hobbies.

Traditionally, work has filled a large part of peoples' identities - too large, some would argue. A witness to that belief is the 50 year-old man, for example, who is suddenly forced to take early retirement, and who, despite being financially secure, experiences a powerful personal crisis. Who is he without his job title and work? Suddenly he has time to spend with his children, only to find that they have grown up and he really does not even know them. His wife of 25 years has her own life and is not about to give it up suddenly to spend all her time with him. He never did get around to developing those hobbies he talked about, nor has he ever made time for fitness. With work gone, this man's identity is severely shaken.

Your work experience is unlikely to mirror his, as the days of working for the same organization for 25 years appear to be over. However, without careful planning, your personal experience could be similar to his.

Now is the time to begin to think about how you want to spend those 72 hours available to you outside of work and sleep. What would you like your priorities to be? When do you plan to see friends and family? When do you plan to go to the movies, the theatre, go skiing, play squash, run, work-out, read, build, do crafts? Where does education or training fit in?

Start to think about how you spend your time and how you *want* to spend your time. Make plans to incorporate being with people you like, having fun and staying fit into your life. Set priorities for work, family and yourself. List your top three priorities:

1. _____
   _____

2. _____
   _____

3. _____

   _____

Now look at those priorities and calculate the amount of time you spend on each. Do your priorities receive the amount of time they deserve? Or is your third priority receiving most of your time while your largest priority suffers?

Go back to this exercise every six months or so and check on how well you are balancing your priorities. Revisit the question of how well you are integrating family, friends, fitness and fun into your life. If you find that you are spending an inordinate amount of your time on work, assess how much of that is due to poor time management and how much is simply the nature of the work. If it appears to be the latter, sit down and think about whether at this point in your life you are willing to live with a lack of balance. If the answer is yes, continue working as hard, but reassess regularly. If it is no, begin to think about a change.

MANAGING YOUR CAREER

The media have filled their pages during the past few years with gloom-and-doom statements about down-sizing, out-sourcing, flattening hierarchies, re-engineering and the jobless recovery . You're about to enter the changing workplace. These headlines have done little for your peace of mind.

What can **you** do to effectively manage your career despite the gloom and doom? First, *own* your career. Take full responsibility for it. Treat it as you would a company you owned. Thoroughly understand its product - you! Be prepared to market its uniqueness - your skills and experience. Continuously examine the marketplace and ensure that you are competitive. Upgrade skills as necessary. Plan financially. Develop your transition skills.

According to Thomas A. Stewart, in an article in *Fortune*, you should "chart your contribution, not your position. Careers will be defined less by companies (I work for IBM) and more by professions (I design RISC chips); they will be shaped less by hierarchies and more by markets. There are new rules for success and new warning signs of trouble. But when risks are higher, potential rewards are too."[8]

John Kotter, a Harvard business school professor, in his just released book, *The New Rules,* lists eight rules he believes will enhance success in the new workplace:

1. Do not rely on convention; career paths that were winners for most of this century are often no longer providing much success
2. Keep your eyes on globalization and its consequences
3. Move toward the small and entrepreneurial and away from the big and bureaucratic
4. Help big business from the outside as well as on the inside
5. Do not just manage; now you must also lead
6. Wheel and deal if you can
7. Increase your competitive drive
8. Never stop trying to grow; lifelong learning is increasingly necessary for success

Learning to effectively manage your career is just another skill you are capable of developing. Your organization no doubt has a mission statement. Annually, you will probably be asked to establish goals for the upcoming year. If it makes sense professionally, why not try it for yourself. Write a personal mission statement describing how you would like your life to be. Establish measurable objectives that cover all aspects of your life: personal, work, life-style, monetary, volunteerism, fitness - and remember the importance of balance. Write a one-year action plan for each area of your life. Review the plan after six months and again at the end of the year. Then reassess your mission statement. Is it still relevant? If not, rewrite it. Establish new objectives, and this time write a five-year plan.

CONCLUSION

Again, congratulations on attaining your new position. Your career is off to a great start. You have the skills, experience, education and personality to make your position work and work well. I hope this chapter has provided additional tips.

If the experts are right, your new position is just the first of many you will hold throughout your career. Take full advantage of the learning available to you. Keep your eyes open - your next position might be staring you in the face some day. Be prepared, keep your résumé up-to-date, and continually assess what is happening in the marketplace. In today's marketplace, we can no longer rely on institutions for employment security. Self-reliance must replace institutions. Take responsibility for planning for potential periods of unemployment and for retirement. Such planning is essential, and the time to start is now!

A final word: success now and into the twenty-first century will depend on the on-going development of skills, the wise use of them, financial planning and a well-balanced life. Success is yours for the taking. Good luck in your new work!

NOTES

1. Nuala Beck and Joseph Connolly, "Jobs with a Future," *Engineering Dimensions*, Janauary/February 1995.
2. The Toronto *Globe and Mail*, April 10, 1995.
3. Janis Foord Kirk, "Career Monitor," *The Toronto Star*, March 2, 1991.
4. Gordon Powers, "Pack Your Resumes with Punch," *Globe and Mail*, May 13, 1995.
5. *Globe and Mail*, April 29, 1995.
6. Thomas A. Stewart, in *Fortune*, March 20, 1995.
7. *Fortune*, October 13, 1994.
8. Thomas A. Stewart, in *Fortune*, March 20, 1995.

BIBLIOGRAPHY

Chapter 1

Skills Are Your Passport, Edmonton, Alberta Career Development and Employment, 1988

Employability Skills Profile: The Critical Skills Required of the Canadian Workforce, Ottawa, Conference Board of Canada, 1991

Careering and Re-Careering for the 1990's: The Complete Guide to Planning Your Future, Ronald L. Krannich, Woodbridge, VA, Impact Publications, 1993

A Career Success Formula: Career = Work + Leisure, Carl McDaniels, Deborah Hedrick, and Gale Watts, Garett Park, Garett Park Press, 1991

College Majors and Careers: A Resource Guide for Effective Life Planning, Paul Phifer, Garett Park, Garett Park Press, 1993

If You Knew Who You Were...You Could Be Who You Are! Your Comprehensive Personal Career Profile, G.M. Sturman, Woodstock, Bierman House, 1991

Chapter 2

The Nitty Gritty Resume Guide, Annex Resume Centre, 1991

How to Write a Winning Resume, Deborah Perlmutter Bloch, VGM Career Horizons, 1991

Resumes that Mean Business, David Eyler, Random House, 1993

Your First Resume, Ron Fry, Career Press, 1992

The Perfect Resume Strategies, Tom and Ellen Jackson, Doubleday, 1992

The College Student's Resume Guide, Kim Marino, Ten Speed Press, 1992

Developing a Professional Vita or Resume, Carl McDaniels, Garrett Park Press, 1990

The Damn Good Resume Guide, Yana Parker, Ten Speed Press, 1989

The 90 Minute Resume: For Job Hunters Who Want Top-Notch Results Fast, Petersons Guides, 1990

The Guide to Basic Resume Writing, VGM Career Horizons, 1991

Resume Power, Tom Washington, Mount Vernon Press, 1993

Electronic Resume Revolution; Create a Winning Resume for the New World of Job Searching, John Wiley and Sons, 1994

Chapter 3

Environmental Career Guide, N. Basta, John Wiley & Sons, 1991

Ecopreneuring: The Complete Guide to Small Business Opportunities for the Environmental Revolution, Steven J. Bennett, John Wiley & Sons, 1991

Career Explorations, Copp Clark Longman, 1992

Great Jobs for Foreign Language Majors, Julie DeGalan & Stephen Lambert, VGM Career Horizons, Copp Clark Longman, 1994

Make Your Own Breaks: Become an Entrepreneur & Create Your Own Future, Jim Lang, Trifolium Books Inc., 1994

Network Your Way to Your Next Job.....Fast, Clyde C. Lowstuter and David P. Robertson, McGraw-Hill Inc., 1995

Exploring Careers In...., Rosen Publishing, Saunders Book Co., 1988

Careers for the Future, Judy Ross, D.C. Heath Canada LTD., 1992

Information Interviewing: What Is It and How to Use It in Your Career, Martha Stoodley, Garrett Park Press, 1990

Careers for Today Series, Franklin Watts, Nelson Canada, 1991

Career Connections: Great Careers For People..., Weigl Educational Publishers, 1993-1994

Chapter 4

The Perfect Follow-up Method to Get the Job, Jeffrey Allen, J. Wiley & Sons, 1991

Finding a Job in Your Field: A Handbook for Ph.D.'s and M.A.'s, Rebecca Anthony and Gerald Roe, Petersons Guides, 1984

What Color is Your Parachute? A Practical Manual for Job Hunters and Career Changers, Richard Nelson Bolles, Ten Speed Press, 1993

Landing on Your Feet, Mara Brown, McGraw-Hill Ryerson, 1992

The Job Hunters Final Exam, Thomas M. Camden, Surrey Books, 1990

Researching Your Way to a Good Job: How to Find and Use Information on Industries, Companies, Jobs, Careers, Karmen N.T. Crowther, John Wiley & Sons, Inc., 1993

The Quick Job Search, J. Michael Farr, JIST, 1989

The Complete Job Search Handbook, Howard Figler, Henry Holt and Company, 1988

How to Get the Job You Want in Tough Times, Julianne Foler, RGA Publishing, 1991

Part-time Careers: For Anyone Who Wants More Than Just a Job - But Less Than a 40 Hour Work Week, Joyce Hadley, Career Press, 1993

The Academic Job Search Handbook, Mary Morris Heiberger & Julia Miller Vick, University of Pennsylvania Press, 1992

Not Just Another Job, Tom Jackson, Times Books, 1992

The Perfect Job Search, Tom Jackson, Doubleday, 1992

Interview Express, Tom Jackson and Bill Buckingham, Random House, 1993

The Temp Track, Peggy O'Connell Justice, Petersons, 1994

Electronic Job Search: Win with the New Technology that's Reshaping Todays Job Market, Joyce Lain Kennedy, J. Wiley & Sons, 1994

In Search of the Perfect Job: 12 Proven Steps for Getting the Job You Really Want, C.C. Lowstuter & D. Robertson, McGraw-Hill, 1992

Making the Most of the Temporary Employment Market, Karen Mendenhall, Betterway Books, 1993

Jobs for English Majors and Other Smart People, John L. Munschauer, Petersons Guides, 1991

A Big Splash in a Small Pond: Finding a Great Job in a Small Company, R.L. Resnick, Fireside, 1994

Making Contact, Barry Siskind, Macmillan Canada, 1995

Temp: How to Survive and Thrive in the World of Temporary Employment, Deborahann Smith, Shambhala, 1994

The Right Place at the Right Time: Finding a Job in the 1990s, Robert Wegmann & Robert Chapman, Ten Speed Press, 1990

Work in the New Economy: Careers and Job Searching into the 21st Century, Robert Wegman, Robert Chapman, Miriam Johnson, Olympus Publishing, 1989

Job Search Strategies for People with Disabilities, M.A. Witt, Petersons Guides, 1992

Resumes Don't get Jobs: The Realities and Myths of Job Hunting, Bob Weinstein, McGraw-Hill, 1993

Hire Power: The 6-step Process to Get the Job You Need in 60 days - Guaranteed!, Irv Zuckerman, Putnam, 1993

Chapter 5

Life Balance, Linda & Richard Eyre, Ballantine Books, 1987

Shifting Gears, Carole Hyatt, Simon & Schuster, 1990

How to Survive Your First 90 Days at a New Company, Paul Kaponya, A Career Press Book, 1990

Careering and Re-careering for the 90's, Dr. Ronald L. Krannich, Impact Publications, 1993

The Time Trap, Alec Mackenzie, Amacon, 1990

The Changing Workplace, Carl McDaniels, Jossey-Bass Publications, 1989

You Don't Have To Go Home From Work Exhausted, Ann McGee-Cooper with Duane Trammel & Barbara Lau, Bowen & Rogers, 1990

Put Work in its Place, Bruce O'Hara, Work Well Publications, 1988

Take This Job and Love It, Dennis T. Jaffe & Cynthia D. Scott, A Fireside Book, 1988

How to Survive & Thrive in the World of Temporary Employment, Deborahann Smith, Shambhala, 1994

Transitions, Stephen Strasser & John Sena, the career Press, 1990

The Career Doctor, Neil M. Yeager, Ed.D., John Wiley & Sons, Inc., 1991

INDEX